In the Heart of the Bitter-Root Mountains:

The Story of
"the Carlin Hunting Party"

September-December, 1893

In the Heart of the Bitter-Root Mountains:

The Story of "the Carlin Hunting Party"

September-December, 1893

BY
HECLAWA

ILLUSTRATED

G. P. PUTNAM'S SONS

New York
27 WEST TWENTY-THIRD STREET

London
24 BEDFORD STREET, STRAND

The Knickerbocker Press

1895

COPYRIGHT, 1894
BY
G. P. PUTNAM'S SONS
Entered at Stationers' Hall, London

Printed and Bound by
The Knickerbocker Press, New York
G.P PUTNAM'S SONS

*TO
WILLIAM P. CARLIN
BRIGADIER-GENERAL, U.S.A.
THIS VOLUME IS GRATEFULLY
DEDICATED*

ISBN: 978-1-6673-0539-4 paperback
ISBN: 978-1-6673-0540-0 hardcover

Contents

PREFACE 9

INTRODUCTION 12

CHAPTER I. The clearwater country and the lo-lo trail 19

CHAPTER II. The equipment 26

CHAPTER III. On the lo-lo trail 33

CHAPTER IV. The lost indian prospect 45

CHAPTER V. In camp 50

CHAPTER VI. The first elk 55

CHAPTER VII. A hunt at the upper warm springs 60

CHAPTER VIII. Snowed in 68

CHAPTER IX. A hunt at the lower warm springs 76

CHAPTER X. Building the rafts 84

CHAPTER XI. A reverie 94

CHAPTER XII. The Journey Down The Kooskooskee 96

CHAPTER XIII. The rescue and disbandment 130

CONCLUSION 140

Appendix a. The relief expeditions 142

Appendix b. The phenomenal precipitation of rain and snow in the fall of 1893 ... 148

Appendix c. The colgate searching parties 151

Appendix d. Biographical 156

Appendix e. A few hints relative to suitable arms for big-game shooting ... 162

Appendix f. Some press accounts 167

Appendix g. Lewis and clark's journey through the clearwater country ... 175

IN THE HEART OF THE BITTER-ROOT MOUNTAINS:
The Story of "the Carlin Hunting Party"

> To sit on rocks and muse o'er flood and fell
>   To slowly trace the forest's shady scene
> Where things that own not man's dominion dwell
>   And mortal foot hath ne'er or rarely been;
> To climb the trackless mountain all unseen,
>   With the wild flock that never needs a fold
> Alone o'er steeps and foaming falls to lean;
>   This is not solitude; tis but to hold
> Converse with Nature's charms,
>   and view her stores unrolled.
>
>   -- CHILDE HAROLD.

PREFACE

In submitting this little volume to the reading public, the author is fully conscious of the fact that he is adding another to the vast number of books on hunting and kindred subjects with which the book-stores are already flooded. Then, too, the party, of whose experiences this is the authorized account, suffered a most painful misfortune, which it seemed could best be healed over by refraining from embodying the unfortunate circumstances in permanent form. The many friends of the author, however, argued otherwise, and the result is the production of this volume.

The purpose of this work, like many others of the same class, is to bring to the home and fireside some of the freshness, the novelty, and the excitement of a sojourn in a vast wilderness, such as can no longer be paralleled in the eastern United States or Europe. Descriptions true to nature, facts and correct ideas concerning the woods, practical hints on the art of hunting, and expedients for avoiding and overcoming difficulties, are, it is hoped, some of the valuable features to be found in this work.

In hunting trips, and especially in those undertaken for recreation and pleasure solely, the most democratic principles are observed. When intimate friends comprise the party, the utmost familiarity and ingenuousness invariably prevail, which constitute the real charm of camp life. In keeping, therefore, with the character and purpose of the hunting party, and to reflect as faithfully as possible the realities of life in the woods, the author has endeavored to relate the story of the party in a literal and very informal manner.

All the illustrations in this work will be found to be accurate and reliable, having been reproduced directly from photographs.

The author is justified in referring, with much gratification, to the new map of the Clearwater country and contiguous territory. It may be a surprise to many, but it is a fact nevertheless, that no accurate map of that district is in existence, none even that gives correctly the relative location and importance of the principal water-courses. Although the accompanying map is partly a sketch, it was prepared with much care from all the reliable data which a careful study of the history of the region has developed, and gives for the first time an approximate idea of the main topographical features of the basin of the Clearwater River. It is to be greatly regretted that the name Clearwater has almost entirely superseded that of Kooskooskee. In justice to Lewis and Clark, who first explored the stream and designated it by its Indian name, the river, from its source near the headwaters of the St. Joseph to its mouth at Lewiston, should be called Kooskooskee.

The author takes much pleasure in acknowledging his indebtedness to Francis P. Harper and Elliott Coues for their exceptional liberality in permitting a reprint of a portion of their edition of THE HISTORY OF THE LEWIS AND CLARK EXPEDITION to the Pacific Ocean.

The formal as well as the grateful acknowledgments of the author are tendered to Capt. John Mullan, U. S. A., for his deep interest and valuable assistance in producing the map of the Clearwater country; to Lieut. James A. Leyden, U. S. A., for an accurate map of Lake Coeur d'Alene; to Major-Gen. O. O. Howard, Brig.-Gen. R. N. Batchelder, and Lieut. Charles P. Elliott, of the U. S. A., and Martin P. Spencer, J. P. M. Richards, C. S. Penfield, John Gaffney, F. M. Hinds, and M. C. Normoyle, for information and data relative to the Clearwater country and the Lo-Lo trail; to William H. Wright for the history of the relief expedition sent out from Fort Missoula, and many interesting photographs; to James W. Howard, H. C. Hayward, and Guy Norton, for personal favors, and to the Rev. S. A. Ziegenfuss for a patient and critical reading of the manuscript.

In behalf of the "Carlin Hunting Party," the author takes this opportunity to express the most sincere thanks and grateful appreciation of the party to Brig.-Gen. W. P. Carlin, who, when the party was over-due, and deep snow had fallen prematurely in the mountains, became solicitous for their safety, organizing and sending out four relief expeditions, one of which successfully accomplished its rescue. The party will always be deeply indebted and sincerely grateful to Lieut. Charles P. Elliott, U.S.A., in command of the successful expedition, and his brave, hardy men for their indefatigable efforts, and the hardships and exposure they suffered on the expedition, as well as for the uniform courtesy and kindness they manifested toward them during the journey down the Clearwater River. The thanks of the party are tendered also to the officers and men of the other expeditions, who suffered similar hardships and were denied even the small satisfaction of finding the party sought.

Many other persons are named in the course of the narrative who in various ways favored and befriended the party, and who will always be remembered with a feeling of profound gratitude.

INTRODUCTION

WHILE every child is familiar with the geography of the United States and can sketch from memory a map of the Northwestern States, very few persons possess definite and accurate ideas of their great size and the diversified character of the earth's surface within their boundaries. Nor can anyone who has always lived in the more densely populated districts of the world, surrounded by the comforts and conveniences of our modern civilization, appreciate or comprehend the dangers, difficulties and privations experienced by those bold, hardy men who first explored and settled that region.

Since the advent of the transcontinental railways, much of the "wild and woolly" character of the great West has disappeared. The railways have opened to the world immense agricultural and mining districts, into which great streams of cosmopolitan humanity are constantly flowing. So rapid, in fact, has been the influx of immigrants that, with the admission of the new States into the Union with the requisite population, the mistaken conclusion has been drawn that the region is "settled up." On the contrary, only the most easily accessible places – the valleys of the principal water-courses – have as yet been touched by civilization.

The vast size of the new States will explain this. Take Montana and Idaho, for example. These two States represent an area larger than the German Empire, more than three times as large as the combined area of the New England States, and over twice as large as the Middle States. Thirty hours are consumed by the fastest through express trains in traversing the State of Montana alone.

Is it surprising, then, that within our own domains, isolated from railways and settlements, protected from the encroachments of the settler by the formidable character of the mountains, the threatening streams, and the almost impenetrable forests, there should be vast regions, primitively beautiful, which the eye of the explorer alone has as yet discovered?

To every busy man there comes at times a restless feeling – a longing for an indefinable something, a change from the monotonous routine of every-day work. A short sojourn at the seashore, an ocean voyage, a season of travel – each satisfies that longing, but only in a greater or less degree, leaving on the mind a consciousness of something yet lacking, a fond wish unfulfilled. One tires of the gayeties and frivolities of fashionable life at the seaside and mountain resorts; the ocean grows wearisome after a few days, and constant travel wears upon one until, tired and full of fads and caprices, the man of cosmopolitan tastes is dissatisfied with everything and imagines himself always uncomfortable.

But to him who loves the woods and all that they contain, to whom " the fountains murmur and the rills sing," who finds "tongues in trees" and "sermons in stones," who can spend hours in mute admiration of Nature in her wildest moods – to him, despite the fatigue and difficulties of the undertaking, a "hard trip" into some almost inaccessible region affords perfect enjoyment. To live for a season a primitive life, in close contact with Nature's virgin charms; to forget for a time the petty jealousies and quibbles of our effete, selfish world; to climb lofty mountains, descend into the wildest gulches and deepest canyons; to thrust one's way through dense thickets of brush and brier, over and around ragged ledges of rock; to navigate swift waters and sail serenely the placid blue expanse of a wood-bordered lake, – combining, in short, the absorbing interest of exploration with the excitement of the chase – oh, who can describe the freedom, the exhilaration, the *abandon* of such an existence!

Under these favorable conditions, health comes as a "by-product," and one returns from such an outing satisfied, happy, and refreshed in mind and body.

IN THE HEART
OF THE BITTER-ROOT
MOUNTAINS

CHAPTER I.

THE CLEARWATER COUNTRY AND THE LO-LO TRAIL

HIGH on the western slope of the Bitter-Root Mountains of eastern Idaho, hundreds of miniature streams dash their foaming waters fresh from fields of perpetual snow into four main forks which form the headwaters of the Clearwater River. Skirting the bases of lofty mountains, surging against the naked faces of projecting cliffs, leaping over precipices, and ever and anon struggling with innumerable boulders planted firmly in their beds, – the roaring forks of the Clearwater River follow their sinuous course westward. Scores of creeks and branches, draining a territory thousands of square miles in area, add constantly to their volume. These tributaries have for ages been eroding the solid granite. Deep gulches and canyons have been formed, many miles in extent, converting the whole region into a wild, tangled mass of irregular mountain ranges and spurs, whose ragged crests and peaks tower to altitudes of four to eight thousand feet above the sea. The less precipitous slopes are covered with a dense growth of pine, fir, cedar and tamarack, while many steep hillsides with northern exposures have impenetrable thickets of pine and fir saplings. Occasionally, large rockbound areas are found, covered with moosebrush, and here and there, sometimes clinging to almost vertical hillsides and often occupying the tiny flats nestling by the sides of the tortuous water-courses, are dense patches of brush, yielding in their season a profusion of berries.

This veritable wilderness, whose forests abound in game, and whose streams teem with trout, covers an area equal to that of the State of West Virginia. It can boast of not having a single permanent habitation of man, not even a wagon road. The Lo-Lo trail, now almost abandoned and so poorly denned that only expert woodsmen and guides can follow it, is the best route by which this region may be entered or traversed. On account of the exceptionally rough character of the country, the trail, instead of following the watercourses, as is usually the case, follows the undulating and convoluted crests of ridges, often requiring ascents and descents of several thousand feet. Into these wilds the whistle of the locomotive has never penetrated; their pristine solitudes are undisturbed by the ring of the settler's axe; even the wandering Indian hesitates before risking a journey into the mountain fastnesses, and bold indeed is the occasional prospector or hunter who ventures into their unexplored depths.

The Indians were, of course, the original explorers of this wild region, and there are, in the more accessible localities, unmistakable evidences of their early presence. Whether they had permanent villages or remained for any considerable periods of time in those localities is, of course, unknown; but the rigorous climate, and the excessive snowfall to which the district is subject during the winter months, probably drove them out of the mountains at that season.

The first white men who visited the Clearwater country were Lewis and Clark, who traversed it in their famous exploring expedition to the Pacific Ocean in 1805-6. It is most interesting to observe that their notes and descriptions of the country as found in their original narrative are as fresh and true to nature as when they were first penned.

After the exit of Lewis and Clark, the Rocky Mountain region of Montana and Idaho was not revisited by white men for forty-seven years. At the expiration of that period – in 1853 – the explorations and surveys "to ascertain the most practicable and economical route for a railroad from the Mississippi River to the Pacific Ocean" were begun, under the direction of the War Department. Four principal parties were organized* and sent into the field, each being assigned a certain territory in which to operate. Isaac I. Stevens, Governor of Washington (the General Stevens who was killed at Chantilly in 1862), was placed in charge of one of these parties, and it was in the prosecution of this work that A. W. Tinkham, C. E., in 1853, and Lieut. John Mullan, in 1854, traversed the Clearwater country from east to west, following approximately the old southern and northern Nez Perces trails respectively. Lieutenant Mullan subsequently (1858-1802) was engaged in the exploration, location, and construction of a military wagon road from Fort Benton on

---

* see Appendix, p. 223 ???

IN THE HEART OF THE BITTER-ROOT MOUNTAINS:
The Story of "the Carlin Hunting Party"

the Missouri River to Fort Walla Walla on the Columbia River. The necessary examination of the intervening territory — which embraces the Clearwater basin — in order to solve the problem of location intelligently, involved an enormous amount of the most difficult and laborious exploration. Referring to the character of this locality, Captain Mullan recently said: "I have travelled over much of the Rocky Mountain region from the 39th to the 49th degree of latitude north, and from the plains of the Missouri to the plains of the Columbia, but nowhere did I ever meet with so difficult, rugged, severe, and broken or mountainous country as that situated between the Tinkham route of 1853, and the Coeur d'Alene route (by me) in 1854."

For many years the vast region comprising the St. Joseph, the Clearwater, and the Salmon River basins and the main range of the Bitter-Root Mountains formed an impassable barrier between the settlements east and west of it. The necessity of opening a more direct line of communication between Virginia City, Mont., and Lewiston, Idaho, than the Mullan road afforded, caused the Government in 1866 to make an appropriation of fifty thousand dollars for that purpose. The same year a reconnoissance was made and the route located by Wellington Bird, assisted by George B. Nicholson, C. E., and Oliver Marcy. It was soon ascertained that the character of the country was such that the appropriation in hand was barely sufficient to open a good trail suitable for the passage of pack trains. The evident desirability of even so unpretentious a thoroughfare led to its immediate construction, and the following year the trail was completed. The route selected was, briefly, as follows: From Lewiston over already

CHAPTER I. THE CLEARWATER COUNTRY AND THE LO-LO TRAIL

existing wagon roads on the south side of the Clearwater River to Schultz's (now Greer's) Ferry; from that point a trail was graded eastward, following approximately the old northern Nez Perces trail, which, at a distance of from ten to twenty-five miles, parallels the Kooskooskee to the main range of the Bitter-Root Mountains. The trail there crosses the headwaters of the Kooskooskee, passes thence over the Bitter-Root range at Lo-Lo pass, and descends the eastern slope of the mountains along the Lou-Lou fork of the Bitter-Root River in Montana to Fort Missoula. Near that point the trail intersected Mullan's military wagon road, along which and other previously constructed roads the route led to Virginia City. That portion of the route between Schultz's Ferry and Fort Missoula became known as the Lo-Lo trail, taking its name from a creek of that name, which empties into the Clearwater River from the north. As civilization has advanced, those portions of the Lo-Lo trail from Missoula to the Lou-Lou Warm Springs on the east, and from Greer's Ferry to the Mussel-Shell Creek on the west, have been superseded by wagon roads. The total length of the trail from Weippe, the last settlement at the present time on the west, to Missoula, is about one hundred and thirty miles.

After the Northern Pacific Railroad was built along the Clark's fork of the Columbia River, a better means of communication between points east and west of the Clearwater country was secured by that route, and the Lo-Lo trail, though more direct, fell into disuse.

During the Nez Perces war in 1877, after Gen. O. O. Howard had defeated Chief Joseph at White Bird canyon, that chieftain and his remnant of hostile Indians retreat-

IN THE HEART OF THE BITTER-ROOT MOUNTAINS:
The Story of "the Carlin Hunting Party"

ed northward, crossed the Clearwater River, and passed over the Lo-Lo trail to the Bitter-Root River in Montana. The pursuit of the Indians through this region involved difficulties which the uninitiated cannot comprehend.*

A brief extract from General Howard's interesting work, "Chief Joseph," will serve to assist the reader to form an idea of the country and the condition of the trail, only ten years after it had been built:

"It does not appear far to the next peak. It is not so in a straight course, but such a course is impossible. 'Keep to the hog-back!' That means there is usually a crooked connecting ridge between two neighboring mountain heights and you must keep on it. The necessity of doing so often made the distance three times greater than by straight lines; but the ground was too stony, too steep, the canyon too deep, to attempt the shorter course. Conceive this climbing ridge after ridge, in the wildest kind of wilderness, with the only possible pathway filled with timber, small and large, crossed and cris-crossed; and now, while the horses and mules are feeding on innutritious wiregrass, you will not wonder at 'only sixteen miles a day.'

"'Didn't the hostile Indians go there?' the reader inquiries. Yes; they jammed their ponies through, up the rocks, over, and under, and around the logs and among the fallen trees, without attempting to cut a limb, leaving blood to mark their path; and abandoned animals, with broken legs, or 'played out,' or stretched dead by the wayside.

"Our guide, Chapman, says, in frontier parlance, 'No man living can get so much out of a horse like an Indian can.' Had we, for three days along the Lo-Lo trail, fol-

---
* Originally Oyipe.

lowed closely the hostiles' unmerciful example, we would not then have had ten mules left on their feet fit to carry our sugar, coffee, and hard-bread. ... At half-past five A.M., Spurgin, with his axemen, was already on the trail, working hard to get ahead of the command, so that it might make, to-day, the utmost distance over this terribly rough and obstructed pathway. He cleared away the fallen trees, made bridges across chasms, and when there was time, by side-digging or walling with fragments of the rock, he improved portions of the break-neck trail."

Sixteen years have elapsed since the Nez Perces outbreak, and the Lo-Lo trail, becoming yearly more and more obstructed, exists now only in history, for it is almost obliterated and practically abandoned. The region it traversed has relapsed again into its primitive state – a vast unbroken wilderness, thrillingly interesting in its history and traditions, and impressively beautiful in its bold, majestic scenery. Far removed from the outposts of civilization; the water-courses impracticable for boats or canoes; and the region practically inaccessible except by the difficult Lo-Lo trail, with an expensive equipment, – the basin of the Clearwater River, with its vast forests, dense thickets, and innumerable streams, will remain for many years to come a natural and ideal home for large game, – a safe and quiet retreat – a haven where the native denizens of the forest need have no fear of molestation.

CHAPTER II.

THE EQUIPMENT

"It's a 'bird,' and fits me exactly," said Will, referring to his new gun, as soon as the usual handshaking and salutations were over, "and I want you to come right up to our room and see it."

"Wait until you see mine, old man," replied Abe, who had just arrived in Spokane from the East to join Will's hunting party. "It is the best all-around, general-service gun I ever saw," continued Abe; "but let me arrange to have my baggage sent up."

In a half-hour the two intimates were comfortably domiciled in a large room of Hotel Spokane, and were admiring their guns, which had been built especially for the trip.

Will's gun was a three-barrelled paradox, weight under eight pounds, and had been completed only a few weeks previously by one of the leading gunmakers in the country. It had two 12-gauge barrels side by side, paradox-bored (rifled for a few inches in the muzzle, so as to shoot balls accurately), and a 32-calibre rifle-barrel directly underneath the shot-barrels. The rifle-barrel was

CHAPTER II. THE EQUIPMENT

chambered for the popular 32-40-165 Winchester cartridge, while the shot-barrels took the standard- inch paper shell. Will had given a *carteblanche* order for the very best material and workmanship, and the gun maker had exhausted all of Will's patience by consuming fourteen months in its production. But it was a beauty! Balance excellent; locks that worked smoothly and silk-like; the stock the finest Italian walnut; while the workmanship, the lines, fitting, and engraving were simply superb.

Abe's gun was an ordinary 12-gauge Winchester repeating shotgun, into which a paradox-barrel had been fitted, thus converting it into a repeating rifle as well. Both guns were unique, and had been evolved by the two "gun cranks" during the preceding two years. Besides shooting ball, both guns shot shot and buckshot about as well as the average cylinder-bored guns of the same gauge.

"Let me see one of your ball cartridges," said Abe.

"Here's one I cut open yesterday," said Will, producing an ordinary A-grade paper shell, slit its whole length longitudinally and exposing a conical bullet with one groove. Five wads separated the bullet and powder.

"Odd-shaped bullet, isn't it?" said Abe. "But what results did K get with your gun, shooting alternate barrels at two hundred yards?" – referring to a test the gunmaker had agreed to make.

"Will unrolled a large pasteboard target, showing ten shots which had been fired consecutively with alternate barrels at a distance of two hundred yards. The shots were all on a circle eleven and three-quarter inches in diameter, and well bunched in and around an eight-inch bull's-eye.

IN THE HEART OF THE BITTER-ROOT MOUNTAINS:
The Story of "the Carlin Hunting Party"

"Jove, why that's as good as the average hunting rifle will do!" exclaimed Abe. "I thought I would surprise you with the test score of my gun, but yours is just as good, if not better. We never dreamed of getting results like this, did we?"

"It 'knocks out' anything they have ever accomplished across the water with paradox-guns," replied Will.

"The old man evidently knew what he was talking about when he guaranteed to turn out as good paradox-barrels as could be obtained anywhere, although I admit I doubted his ability to do so at the time. But now, what about the trip?" asked Abe.

"Well, I had the hardest work you ever heard of to get reliable information about the game here; but one thing is certain: It is too late to hunt mountain sheep, unless you want to take your chances of getting snowed in. The best trip we can take under the circumstances, so far as I can judge, is to go to the headwaters of the Clearwater in eastern Idaho. A guide I was talking with yesterday guaranteed us shots at elk, and says if not too late we will be sure to get bear there too. He says that there are any quantity of black-tail deer, a few moose, and on the high peaks goats, but that it is too late to go up to the peaks this fall. How would that kind of a trip suit you?"

"You know, Will, that I had set my heart on getting a 'big-horn'," replied Abe. "But if that is out of the question, I'm perfectly satisfied with the trip to the Clearwater country if you are. What have you done about an outfit?"

"Almost nothing. You know that the character of the outfit depends largely upon where we expect to go, and so I had to wait for you. You remember our old cook, Col-

CHAPTER II. THE EQUIPMENT

gate? Well, he is ready to start on a moment's notice. I had him go up to the St. Joe country to see about getting bear dogs, and Palmer kindly sent two of his down yesterday, with this note.' Here Will handed Abe a note reading as follows:

> DEAR CARLIN: —
> I send you two terrier dogs, which we have used with success on bear, etc., on condition that you come up and pay us a visit on your return. Hoping, they may be of service to you, I am most cordially yours,
>
> FRED PALMER.

"Fred is a good one, isn't he?" said Abe, returning the letter. "We're awfully lucky to get those dogs. I tell you, old 'stuff,' we'll have a great hunt yet."

Just then the door opened, and John, the third member of the party, came in. After a few minutes' conversation, Will and Abe went out to see the guide, while John busied himself with some correspondence.

The guide, Martin Spencer, was soon found, and satisfactory arrangements were made with him to guide the party. The three then returned to the hotel to prepare a list of the provisions and camping paraphernalia required for a five-weeks' trip. Colgate had arrived in the meantime, and he and Spencer prepared the following list of provisions:

IN THE HEART OF THE BITTER-ROOT MOUNTAINS:
The Story of "the Carlin Hunting Party"

125 lbs. flour.	5 lbs. dried apples.
30 lbs. breakfast bacon.	5 lbs. dried apricots.
40 lbs. salt pork.	1 gal. maple syrup.
20 lbs. beans.	2 doz. tallow candles.
40 lbs. salt.	3 lbs. laundry soap.
10 lbs. oatmeal.	¼ doz. cakes toilet soap.
10 lbs. cornmeal.	5 lbs. raisins.
30 lbs. sugar.	¼ lb. pepper.
1 lb. tea.	¼ gal. vinegar.
8 lbs. coffee.	A supply of block matches.
2 doz. cans condensed milk.	1 gal. brandy.
3 lbs. baking-powder.	40 lbs. of potatoes (purchased at Weippe later).
Citron, sage, mace, thyme.	
10 lbs. alum.	

Spencer, Will, and Abe prepared the following list of camp equipage:

1 10x12 ft. wall-tent.	9 tin plates.
1 7x7 ft. A-tent.	9 tin cups.
1 large wagon-cover or fly.	¼ doz. teaspoons.
10 double blankets.	¼ doz. dessertspoons.
2 heavy quilts.	2 butcher's-knives.
¼ doz. towels.	2 large spoons.
3 canvas pack-covers, 4x6.	1 large meat-knife.
5 yds. crash.	1 4-lb. axe.
5 yds. heavy unbleached muslin.	1 2-lb. axe.
	1 8-in. flat file.
3 camp-kettles (nested).	1 box assorted copper-wire rivets.
2 gold-pans (for use as dishpans, etc).	
	2 ten-yard coils wire.
1 granite stew-pan.	2 lbs. assorted wire nails.
2 frying-pans.	1 ball coarse twine.
1 reflector (for baking bread).	1 ball light twine.
	50 ft. extra rope.
1 coffee-pot.	1 rubber air-bed.
¼ doz. knives and forks.	1 doz. extra cloth sacks.

CHAPTER II. THE EQUIPMENT

In addition to the guns already mentioned, Spencer took a 40-70-330 Winchester single-shot rifle, with reloading tools and plenty of ammunition. John's arms consisted of a 45-90-300 Winchester repeating rifle, and a Schofield model Smith & Wesson revolver. Will and Abe both had Smith & Wesson Russian model revolvers. A 40-82-260 Winchester repeating rifle was taken as a reserve gun, in case any of the other guns should break down or be in any way disabled on the trip. The whole party was well supplied with fishing-tackle. Will had an Eastman folding camera, with all modern improvements, fitted with an excellent lens. Abe took one of the new "Trokonets," a hand camera, for which a harness had been made, so it could be carried on his back. A screw-driver to take apart guns, gun oil, toilet cases, sewing materials, hunting-knives, tobacco, etc., completed the camp furniture and supplies. Unfortunately, by an oversight, Mr. Palmer had failed to send us the names of the two terriers, and as it was impossible to communicate with him before starting into the woods, the two dogs were named "Idaho" and " Montana" – the names being suggested by the proximity of our proposed hunting-ground to the boundary line between those States. A fine spaniel belonging to Colgate was also taken with us for grouse.

Spencer estimated that five pack-horses would be necessary to carry the provisions, etc.; and, as there were five persons in the party, five saddle-horses with complete trappings were also required. The following day Spencer and Will were delegated to purchase the horses, trappings, etc., Abe to buy the camp equipage, while Colgate attended to the purchase of the groceries and provisions.

In the matter of food, only necessaries were taken, the object being to avoid excessive weight. All the provisions were done up in cloth sacks, to avoid the danger of spilling or losing them. A car had been chartered in the meantime, into which the whole equipment was loaded as fast as purchased, and early the following morning the car left for Kendrick, Idaho, the nearest railway station to the Clearwater country. The party followed an hour later in the passenger train, arriving at Kendrick late in the afternoon. On the arrival of the freight train that evening, the horses were removed from the car to a small enclosure or corral near the railroad siding, and fed. The safety of the balance of the things left in the car was next attended to, after which the party found comfortable accommodations for the night at the St. Elmo Hotel.

CHAPTER III.

ON THE LO-LO TRAIL

SUITABLE arrangements having been made the preceding evening, at dawn on the morning of September 18th a number of the horses were taken to the blacksmith-shop to be shod. While that operation was in progress all the camp equipage and provisions were arranged into packages of convenient form and weight, called "packs," and lashed to the horses as fast as they were shod. At one o'clock of the same day all the final preparations were completed and the caravan, or "outfit" – to use the Western term – started for the mountains. The whole party was in excellent spirits, and the easy fourteen-mile ride to Snell's mill, through a rolling farming country, was very much enjoyed. We halted just at sundown. Supper was soon ready, and was partaken of with much relish by the light of the camp-fire. Mr. Snell kindly gave us permission to sleep in his barn, and all passed a comfortable night, with newly mown hay for a bed.

The next day we started off bright and early. The Nez Perces Indian reservation was entered before noon. A few

IN THE HEART OF THE BITTER-ROOT MOUNTAINS:
The Story of "the Carlin Hunting Party"

hours later the party crossed the North Fork of the Clearwater on a ferryboat operated by Indians. From the North Fork the route led along the Clearwater River for several miles, and then ascended the high mountain on the north side of the river. Camp was made near the summit at about four o'clock in the afternoon. After the packs and saddles had been removed from the horses, Abe started out with Daisy for some grouse, and returned in about an hour with three, which were prepared for supper.

The following morning, September 20th, it was cloudy, and several light showers during the forenoon made the riding very disagreeable. At noon the party reached Weippe, where forty pounds of potatoes were purchased from Mr. Gafney. The journey was then resumed through open glades and strips of timber to Brown's Creek. Here an old cabin furnished excellent shelter, as it was raining when the party arrived there. Several grouse had been killed during the day by Will and Abe, which were enjoyed at the evening meal.

The next morning it was raining hard. Consequently, it was decided to remain at the cabin that day. In the middle of the forenoon, however, Will and Abe became impatient; the former got his fly-book and said he was going to try the trout in the little brook, and the latter took his gun to see if any grouse could be found. John also sallied out in quest of grouse, taking his revolver. In about an hour's time Will returned to the cabin with fifty-three trout, a quarter-pound to one and a half pounds in weight, and reported rare sport in taking them. The stream was so small that he had cut a willow switch about seven feet

CHAPTER III. ON THE LO-LO TRAIL

long, and, with only four feet of line, had been able to take in an hour all we could use. Abe and John returned to the cabin at noon with only two grouse each.

That afternoon a man who had come over to Brown's Creek to drive out some cattle called at our camp. He was a typical mountain rancher, wearing a "slicker" and "chaps," and a large wide-brimmed hat. On his pony, or "cayuse," he carried a week's supply of provisions, a gun, and an axe. Hitching his "cayuse" to the fence, he approached the cabin, and, seeing Spencer, who was outside at the time, he addressed him with:

"Hello, pardner, you struck a pretty good camp here on a rainy day, didn't yez?"

Spencer, surmising the man to be the possible owner of the cabin, was very polite, and explained the situation and the circumstances which led to our taking possession of the cabin. The rancher then said:

"Oh, you fellers is all right. I reckon if [the owner of the cabin] was here, he'd make you go inter the new cabin yander. But say, hain't you the man what took an outfit into the mountains last fall?"

Spencer replied that he had taken a party last fall over the same route we were travelling, and stated about the time they "had passed through there.

"I tho't I'd seed you afore," said the rancher, and then he related the circumstances, which Spencer remembered. This put them on the ground of old acquaintances, and after a few minutes' conversation relative to the last year's trip, the rancher said:

"I reckon you'll have a hard time in the snow, so late in the fall."

"We got out last year all right as late as the 20th of October," said Spencer; "and we figure on getting out this time by the 15th."

"It's a pretty tough trip for tenderfeet," he continued. "Do you fellers all think you can stand the trip?" he asked, turning toward Will, and assuming that the whole party except the guide were unused to the woods.

"Oh! I think we'll 'pull through' all right," said Will, who then directed the conversation to the subject of hunting.

The various kinds of game and the best places in the region were discussed for a half hour or more, when the rancher departed, accepting a dozen trout, which Will offered him.

Soon after his departure, John, who felt some- what piqued at the idea of being taken with the rest of the party for a "tenderfoot," remarked, with considerable feeling: "That man talks as if he thought we were made of sawdust."

READY TO START—CABIN AT BROWN'S CREEK.

CHAPTER III. ON THE LO-LO TRAIL

At about ten o'clock of September 22d, we crossed Mussel-Shell Creek. Up to this time the route had been along a wagon-road, through a sparsely timbered and rolling country, and the travelling was comparatively easy. Here, however, was the terminus of the wagon-road. Forming in single file, with Spencer in the lead, the pack animals were distributed between the riders, and the train continued the journey eastward into the mountains proper over the Lo-Lo trail.

MAKING CAMP—"SNOW SUMMIT."

IN THE HEART OF THE BITTER-ROOT MOUNTAINS:
The Story of "the Carlin Hunting Party"

The character of the country soon changed. The trail led up a steep ascent, passing through dense growths of timber. At about three o'clock we reached-the top of a high ridge called "Snow Summit." Here we found six inches of snow on the ground. Proceeding a little farther, we turned abruptly to the right, and, descending into a neighboring ravine, we came to a glade with a little brook, where we made camp.

The snow was about eight inches deep, but directly around the base of a large cedar at one side of the glade the snow had disappeared. On this limited area of bare ground we piled our "stuff," and set about preparing supper. Although we had not come prepared for winter weather, there was a bountiful supply of blankets, and plenty of excellent firewood near at hand, so that the night was passed without discomfort.

The next day's drive was very difficult and tedious. The trail, besides being steep and crooked, was obstructed by hundreds of fallen trees. Some of these the horses could step over, others they would jump, while those that were too high had to be flanked. In the latter case, it was always necessary to leave the trail, and it was often extremely difficult to get the horses through the dense brush and tangled fallen timber which surrounded these obstructions. Usually the pack-train would follow the leader without much difficulty, but occasionally they would wander off and get "wound up" in the brush and fallen timber so badly, and act so stupidly, that the language which the man who "rounded them up" invariably used was entirely justified.

At about 2 o'clock we reached a glade four miles from Rocky Ridge, where two small streams rise and flow in opposite directions. As it was a journey of five hours to the next desirable camping place, Spencer decided to make camp at this point. Although there was three to five inches of snow on the ground, a space of bare ground was found on the west side of the glade, near several large trees, where a camp was soon established. Everything being suitably disposed for the night, Will went fishing and caught a mess of nice trout in a short time. Will and Abe then went down one stream, while John descended the other for a few hours' hunt. The bag was eight grouse, which, with those killed during the day along the trail, swelled the aggregate to seventeen.

The following day, September 24th, was the hardest day we experienced until we reached our destination. The trail zigzagged up and down steep hillsides, crossed rocky gulches, and skirted or "cross-cutted" steep slopes of loose rock. Occasionally, at bad places, the horses would refuse to go, and it became necessary to dismount and lead and drive them. Sometimes a horse would step into an opening between the rocks and get fast, so that he had to be backed in order that he might release himself. The horses' legs became so badly scratched and bruised that they left bloodmarks in the snow. About noon we arrived at a small stream which had eroded a steep narrow gulch in the side of the mountain. The trail at that point was so rough and uneven that the horses could find no comfortable place to stand, and they became very restless during the ten minutes that we halted to water them and eat our hasty midday lunch. In the afternoon the trail led along steep, open hillsides covered with loose rock, permitting occasionally extended views of the surrounding country, which previously, in the dense forest, had been impossible. That night we reached and camped on Bald Mountain.

IN THE HEART OF THE BITTER-ROOT MOUNTAINS:
The Story of "the Carlin Hunting Party"

ON THE TRAIL NEAR ROCKY RIDGE.

On the maps of this region Bald Mountain is represented as a single, isolated peak. It actually belongs to and forms part of a mountain range. Towering considerably above the surrounding ranges and peaks, with about three-quarters of its top destitute of timber and often covered with snow, it is very conspicuous, and forms a convenient and unmistakable landmark. Before darkness came on, Will, Abe, John, and Spencer walked to its summit to take a look at the surrounding region, and they were amply rewarded. To the north and northwest, spread out before them like an immense map – save that the streams lay hidden deep in their eroded canyons – were the entire basins of the St. Joseph and St. Mary Rivers, while in the more immediate vicinity could be plainly distinguished the basin of the North Fork of the Clearwater. To the south and west were the basins of three other main forks of the Clearwater River. On the east, extending almost from the north to the south and covered with snow, was the main range of the Bitter-Root Mountains boldly outlined against the sky; far off to the south could be seen five of the "Seven Devils," while away in the hazy southwestern horizon were dimly discerned the Blue Mountains of Oregon. Between all these and Bald Mountain, rising to greater or less altitudes, many of them fringed with snow, were an infinite number of ranges, no doubt towering high above the intervening valleys, but dwarfed into insignificance when viewed from Bald Mountain.

We had made our camp near a large, solitary fir tree, under which we expected to sleep, as the night was clear, and it was thought unnecessary to go to the trouble of pitching a tent. It had been our custom after removing the packs and saddles from the horses to hobble one or two of them and leave the others run disencumbered. On this occasion Spencer picketed his powerful white horse with a rope about thirty feet long, tying the end of the rope to a stump. After supper it was quite dark, and all were gathered around the fire. Suddenly a loud tramping was heard, and our hearts almost stopped beating at the thought that the horses had stampeded. Then, like a flash, Spencer's white horse rushed out of the darkness, passed within thirty feet of the campfire, and tore at breakneck speed straight down the steep mountain side into the gloom and darkness below, a piece of the stump skipping and bounding after him at the end of the rope. In a moment all was still. In the excitement, we had imagined the stump to be a cougar in pursuit of the horse, and Will had grabbed his gun to shoot it. Will and Spencer immediately started down the mountain to see what had become of the horse. In about fifteen minutes they returned and reported him safe and sound. He had succeeded in tearing loose from the stump, and miraculously escaped a violent death. Fortunately none of the other horses stampeded, and after recovering Spencer's horse, congratulations were in order on our good fortune in avoiding a stampede, as well as for the opportunity of witnessing the fastest time ever made down so steep an incline. It was a spectacle that will never be forgotten by those who saw it.

The day following – September 25th – the trail led along the high crest of the main divide between the Kooskooskee and the North Fork of the Clearwater, which was covered with snow. A great many bear and deer and several elk tracks were noted as we journeyed along. The elevated position of the trail as we passed from one side to the other of the divide afforded us magnificent views of our surroundings, and the scenery was much enjoyed. From time to time Spencer would point out landmarks and places of interest to the hunter. That evening the Indian "post-offices" (two piles of stone several feet high on each side of the trail) were reached. Turning to the right at that point, we descended about five hundred feet into a gulch, and camped near a spring for the night.

Returning thence to the trail the next morning, we followed it only a short distance, and then turned to the right and took an old Indian trail leading along a burnt ridge down to the Kooskooskee. The last portion of the de-

CHAPTER III. ON THE LO-LO TRAIL

ON THE DIVIDE.

scent was very steep, the trail zigzagging down the nose of a spur, the altitude of which was at least three thousand feet above the river. During this descent Colgate became exhausted, and Will dismounted and assisted him down. On our arrival at the foot of the descent, Colgate's feet and legs were found considerably swollen. His condition alarmed Will very much, and on inquiring into the cause of the swelling and his weakness, Colgate insisted he was simply tired out and would be all right in a day or two, after he would have a little rest.

On reaching the river, all were surprised to find a cabin nearly completed and four men encamped. Spencer went over to the camp, and soon returned with the information that a prospector whom he had known for years, named Jerry Johnson, and a trapper, Ben Keeley, had built the cabin in partnership, packed in plenty of "grub" from Missoula, and were going to spend the winter there. The other two men had come in for a few days' hunting and would return shortly to Missoula.

CHAPTER IV.

THE LOST INDIAN PROSPECT

Six feet in height, with a powerful frame slightly bent by advancing years, black hair mixed with gray, jet black eyes, and a stubbly gray beard – Jerry Johnson, the prospector, would arouse curiosity and interest anywhere.

A Prussian by birth, he emigrated at an early age to New Zealand. There he became interested in mining, and since then he has devoted his life to prospecting for the precious metals in the wildest and most unfrequented regions of the earth, and occasionally acting in the capacity of guide, hunter, and packer. Enthusiastically devoted to his work and often with no other companion than his faithful dog, he has carried pole-pick, axe, and gun and clambered over the mountains under all conditions of weather and climate. For fifteen years he has searched for gold in the most inaccessible regions of the Cascades and the Rocky Mountains, and now, at the advanced age of sixty years, rugged from hardship and exposure, he still loves the isolation and solitude of the mountains and is seeking with characteristic perseverance the long lost Indian Prospect.

IN THE HEART OF THE BITTER-ROOT MOUNTAINS:
The Story of "the Carlin Hunting Party"

JERRY JOHNSON.

Many years ago, while Johnson was encamped in the heart of the Bitter-Root Mountains, a halfstarved Indian found his way to Johnson's camp. The Indian was given food and shelter; and, grateful for the favors shown him, before his departure, in broken English and by signs and gestures, he informed Johnson that he knew where there was "Heap Elk City, heap Pierce City" – meaning much gold, there being mines at the places named. Johnson at once engaged the Indian to guide him to the place. Re-

CHAPTER IV. THE LOST INDIAN PROSPECT

turning to the nearest point where supplies could be purchased, he secured an adequate equipment, and with one other man and the Indian started back into the mountains.

The route taken by the Indian was along the Lo-Lo trail to the Warm Springs. Here the Indian fell sick, but the party pushed on fifteen miles farther east, to a small prairie which Johnson calls "The Park," When they reached this point, the Indian became so sick that he could proceed no farther. Fearing he might die, Johnson got the Indian to tell him how the gold was found. This was quite difficult, as the Indian could speak but a few words of English, and had to convey most of the information by gestures. The story he told was substantially as follows:

A party of Indians were encamped at the place they were journeying to some years previously, and one of them being suddenly taken very sick, a "sweat-bath" was prepared for him.

[An Indian sweat-bath may be thus described: A pool of very cold water is found, either in a spring or brook. A level piece of ground, about five feet in diameter, is then prepared near it, generally on the bank at the edge of the pool. Around the outside edge of this circular piece of ground, pliable willow sticks are stuck into the ground vertically, about eight inches to a foot apart, leaving an opening large enough to pass in and out at the side facing the pool. The tops of these sticks are gathered together at a point about four feet above the ground. Finally a small hollow is dug in the ground on the side opposite the door, and the construction is complete.

When an Indian takes a bad cold or becomes sick from almost any cause, a sweat-bath is invariably prescribed. A number of stones as large as a man's head are heated in a hot fire near the willow arrangement, and several vessels containing plenty of water are placed inside. When the stones are almost red hot, several are taken from the fire and placed in the small hollow referred to, opposite the door. A blanket is then thrown over the willow framework, so as to completely inclose it. Then the Indian strips himself and crawls inside. The heat from the stones, together with the steam formed by dashing water on them, soon excites a profuse perspiration. When this stage is reached, the Indian rushes out of the sweat-bath and plunges into the pool of cold water, where he remains but a few moments – supposedly, just long enough to cool off – after which he scrambles out and imagines himself cured.]

While preparing this sweat-bath, it was necessary to loosen and remove some white rock, and while doing this the Indians discovered that the rock was full of gold, or, as the Indian called it, "Elk City."

The Indian guide grew worse and weaker every hour, and Johnson, being alarmed, took him in his arms and carried him to a more elevated position, where a view to the eastward could be obtained.

"Which way from here?" asked Johnson.

With his remaining strength, the Indian raised his arm and pointed to a peak covered with snow.

"See snow?" he replied. Then raising one finger, he pronounced the single word "sun," and rolled over on his blanket exhausted. A few hours later he died.

Not discouraged by his ill fortune, Johnson and his companion buried the Indian and pushed on to the peak indicated by him, and searched the country beyond and

CHAPTER IV. THE LOST INDIAN PROSPECT

surrounding the peak all that summer, but never succeeded in finding the old Indian camp. Since that time he has spent several summers fruitlessly in the same neighborhood, and is now passing the winter in that desolate snowbound region, hoping, early in the spring, to continue his search for the " Lost Indian Prospect."

CHAPTER V.

IN CAMP

On the north bank of the Kooskooskee, at the edge of a flat or bottom a quarter of a mile in length and averaging a couple of hundred yards in width, in the midst of a young growth of pine and fir trees, we made our camp. At our feet rushed the clear, foaming, roaring waters of the river; while all around us towered the awful mountains, rising to altitudes of from two to four thousand feet above the river, many of them covered with snow and glistening in the bright sunlight. It was a beautiful spot.

But time was precious, and much as we admired our surroundings, we soon gave our attention to matters more practical. The packs were immediately taken from the horses, the saddles removed, and those animals having sore backs had their wounds treated by a healing wash of alum-water. Those likely to stray off were hobbled and turned loose, and then all hands set to work to make camp comfortable. Spencer and Abe put up the wall tent and "fly," and got the "stuff" under shelter, while

CHAPTER V. IN CAMP

the rest busied themselves in unpacking the things and preparing a meal, After dinner a supply of firewood was gotten in, several fir trees were felled and the twigs and needles trimmed from them, for beds. A rude table was constructed under the fly, and before darkness came on we were arranging a programme for the morrow.

During the afternoon one of the two hunters staying at the cabin passed our camp and, stopping, accosted Abe thus:

"Well, pard, how are you making it?"

"Oh, fairly well," replied Abe. "That is a long hill to come down, isn't it?" pointing to the ridge above.

"It's to come down, but it's a to go up. This hull country's full o' slide-rock, and it's the roughest place I'se ever in, I b'lieve."

"What luck did you have with the game?" asked Abe.

"We killed a cow elk at the lower lick the first day; and outside a few chickens, that was all the game I see," replied the man. "How long is you fellers goin' to stay yer?" he asked.

"Oh, about two weeks," Abe replied, "if we have decent luck. How long do you expect to remain?"

"We pull out fer Missoula to-morrer," he replied, "to take some of the hosses out."

"Come over and see us to-night after we get camp ready," said Abe.

"Don't mind if I do," replied the man, as he took a huge chew of tobacco, and started toward the prospector's cabin.

Spencer was to pilot us to the lower warm springs the following morning, so we rose before daybreak. We ate a hearty breakfast, and although it rained, we sallied out just at dawn. A good trail followed along the bank of the river and the hillside, but it was overgrown with brush, which hung, dripping, over it. We were wet to the skin long before we reached the springs, but as wettings are some of the penalties the hunter must often pay for good sport, we kept cheerfully on. When near the springs, Spencer, who was familiar with the locality, took the lead, with Will close behind; but we approached too rapidly, and a deer which had been at the springs to "lick," was scared away before any of us could get a shot.

Spencer gave us some general information concerning the country for a few miles around, to aid us in our future hunting; and after walking a mile farther down the river, we returned, wet and bedraggled, to camp in time for dinner.

In the afternoon Spencer took Will and Abe to the upper warm springs, three miles above. As these were on the other side of the river, three horses were caught and saddled, and as Will and Abe expected to stay all night, blankets and a day's provisions were taken along.

Unfortunately, it continued to rain. After showing them the springs and helping them to dispose of the horses for the night, Spencer made some valuable suggestions relative to the habits of the game in that locality and returned to the main camp, while Will and Abe made a temporary camp under a large white cedar. There were plenty of fresh tracks, and they were much pleased at the outlook for a successful hunt; but it rained all night, and as they could not keep dry or comfortable without a tent, they returned to the main camp about noon of the next day.

CHAPTER V. IN CAMP

A MEAL IN CAMP.

Colgate was found a trifle improved, but not strong enough to attend to his duties; so we all helped to do the cooking and the work about camp.

Day after day it rained, the sky never once clearing off. We knew we could not stay long in any case, so we were compelled to make the best of it, and hunted every day in the rain. As we became more familiar with the locality and the habits of the game, we met with fair success; but the rain interfered greatly with the pleasure of hunting, and the raw, cold air was very uncomfortable. Hunting under these conditions always involved a thorough wetting, and the necessity of moving about, in order to maintain the proper circulation of the blood and avoid taking colds. Much of the time in camp, especially in the evenings, was devoted to the drying of our wet clothing.

IN THE HEART OF THE BITTER-ROOT MOUNTAINS:
The Story of "the Carlin Hunting Party"

The blankets were always damp, and we frequently held them up to the fire before retiring for the night. An adequate supply of firewood, to maintain suitable fires, was usually brought in before dark, at the expense of considerable labor; but with a large, blazing camp-fire and congenial companions, all discomforts were forgotten, and we invariably fell asleep indulging the deluded hope that the morrow would be fair. John, who seemed to be more sensitive to the cold than the rest of the party, did not care to suffer as much exposure, and consequently hunted very little. He was, besides, particularly unfortunate. On one occasion he spied and was within shot of a large band of elk, but lost a shot at them by an accident.

At another time he was walking along the trail without a gun and came suddenly on a bear. He was, however, very successful with smaller game, of which he bagged a large quantity.

CHAPTER VI.

THE FIRST ELK

WE had been in camp for over five days, and had as yet not been fortunate enough to secure any fresh meat. It had rained every day. The game moved about but little, and visited the licks and their drinking-places at night. Will, who was the most experienced hunter of the party, felt assured of this fact, for he had hunted at all times of the day about the springs; and while there were fresh signs, they had evidently been made the night before. On the evening of the fifth day, several fresh signs of elk (*Wapiti*), were seen along the hillsides, and we felt pretty certain that they had either commenced coming down from the high ranges, or that those already in our vicinity had begun to move about regardless of the wet weather. Accordingly, Will determined to visit the lower lick at daylight the following morning, and spend the day in hunting the adjacent sidehills.

He started for the lower lick just at dawn, and returned to camp at about eleven o'clock, carrying a large heart in his hand. The others had been busy all morning making

IN THE HEART OF THE BITTER-ROOT MOUNTAINS:
The Story of "the Carlin Hunting Party"

camp more comfortable; but as soon as Will was seen approaching, every one became at once deeply interested and came forward to meet him. Seeing the heart, Abe asked:

"Well, what is it?"

"Bull elk," said Will, laconically.

"The d – l!" said Abe, taking Will's hand and giving it a warm squeeze of congratulation. "Luck at last, and fresh meat in camp!"

After congratulations all around, Will went into the tent, laid the rifle on the blankets, and began to change his wet clothes.

"But tell us something about it. Has he a nice set of horns?" asked John.

"Six points, and full grown," said Will briefly; adding, "say, out there, I want you people to know I'm hungry!"

By the time Will had changed his wet clothes and hung them on a line near the fire, a hasty meal had been prepared, and when Will seated himself at the table, he gave the following account of his morning's experience:

"As it was raining when I started, and considering the chances of seeing game very slim, I decided to take the 40-82 instead of my paradox. I started on a rapid walk for the lower lick, but the brush along the trail was 'sopping' wet, and I got wet to the skin before going half a mile. On arriving at the grove of cedars in which the spring is situated, I used the utmost caution in approaching the lick, but found it empty. As I stood debating a moment as to what I should do, I heard the clear whistle of a cow, which I judged must be about a hundred and fifty yards below me, on a small flat skirting the river. Slipping quietly along the brow of the hill, I had hardly emerged from

CHAPTER VI. THE FIRST ELK

the timber when the cow trotted slowly past me, not more than thirty yards away, without seeming in the least disturbed by my presence. Hastily getting behind a large tree, I waited for the bull, which I felt confident would follow her. I had not been there more than half a minute when I saw a pair of magnificent antlers moving slowly from right to left in front of me. The head and body were hidden from view, as the bull was walking up a little gully eighty yards away. I did not dare move, for a few jumps would take the bull out of sight in the timber. Although I did not stir, and he could not possibly have scented me, the bull seemed aware that there was some danger at hand, for he suddenly sprang up the side of the gully and stopped in an open clump of trees, and stood as though trying to decide in what direction the danger lay. His neck and shoulders were hidden by intervening trees, but I felt that I must make the best of the shot offered me, and aimed for the liver. At the report of the rifle he gave one bound and disappeared over the brow of the hill. Hastening to the spot, I found his tracks following a well-worn game-trail, which led, slanting, down the hill. There were no signs of blood, but I felt sure that I had hit him. Walking with extreme caution and peering into all the little ravines and thickets, I had gone about half a mile, when, on stooping down and glancing ahead, I saw the elk lying behind a log seventy-five yards distant and looking directly at me.

"Sitting down quietly, I took careful aim at his neck and fired. The elk staggered to his feet and made for the river. Hastily throwing down the lever and inserting a fresh cartridge, I fired for his shoulder. At the shot he went down on his breast, but regained his feet and started off on three legs. The next shot struck him in the neck, and he went down all in a heap. He was not dead, however, and for fear that he might in his struggles break his antlers on the rocks, I finished him with a shot in the neck. My first sensation was a feeling of great satisfaction at killing the finest elk that I had ever seen; my second was a feeling of disgust with the gun for doing it in such a bungling manner. One shot from a proper rifle in the neck or shoulder, where these miserable little hollow-pointed bullets had struck, would have killed him outright. For fully five minutes I sat and admired the fallen monarch: his magnificent curving antlers; his splendid form and sleek, yellowish sides; the fine, long, reddish-black hair of his scalp and neck. Then, on preparing to bleed and dress him, I found that I had forgotten my long-bladed knife in my haste to get away early this morning, and had only a large pocketknife with me. With this, however, I dressed the elk and hastened back to camp."

After congratulations a second time, we all went down with horses to bring up the meat and antlers, Keeley accompanying us to get some fresh meat, of which he and Jerry were in need. On our arrival, we found the usual number of magpies and ravens rapidly making away with the entrails, amid a perfect pandemonium of harsh sounds. When they saw us, they flew into neighboring trees and watched our proceedings.

Having photographed the elk, we skinned and cut him up, and at four o'clock we were ready to start back to camp. It was found that the first bullet had cut his liver almost in two and had lodged under the skin on the other

CHAPTER VI. THE FIRST ELK

side. The second bullet had barely broken one shoulder and smashed into bits on the big bones, failing to penetrate farther. None of the last three bullets had passed through the neck, which was very thick, even for this season of the year.

We started for camp and were overtaken by darkness half a mile beyond the lick. Keeley's horse slipped and rolled down a slippery side-hill, but by dint of considerable swearing and work on the part of his master, the horse was brought back to the trail. The darkness became so intense when a mile from camp that we were forced to build a fire, unpack the horses, and leave the meat and antlers under a tree till morning. The horses being turned loose while the fire was being built, one of them, clumsily, struck against a dead tree, about eight inches in diameter. It fell and just grazed Will's arm – a very fortunate escape from a broken shoulder.

All the matches were used in trying to start the fire, and we had a miserable time stumbling about in the darkness. After floundering around for an hour or so, Keeley came along with a torch made from cedar shavings, and we reached camp about eight o'clock. It took us four hours to go less than four miles. The meat and antlers were secured the first thing in the morning.

CHAPTER VII.

A HUNT AT THE UPPER WARM SPRINGS

It had been raining all morning, and Abe, thoroughly drenched, had just returned from a hunt at the lower lick. He had seen nothing, and looked a trifle disappointed.

"Let's go to the upper lick and stay all night," said Will. "The moon is down at nights now, and there ought to be a good show mornings and evenings."

"I'll go you," said Abe. "As soon as I get on dry things we'll hunt up the horses."

The horses were found grazing on the side of the ridge above the flat, and two of them were soon caught, brought in, and saddled. A double blanket each; a small camp kettle, inside of which were packed two tin cups, two spoons, two tin plates, and a small quantity of salt, coffee, sugar, condensed milk, and bacon; some raw elk-steak, bread, a hand-axe, and some ropes – all were suitably arranged and fastened to the horses. At two o'clock we were ready to start.

The trail led up the river bank, and for a quarter of a mile was lined on both sides by bushes loaded with

CHAPTER VII. A HUNT AT THE UPPER WARM SPRINGS

berries. A little farther on, the steep slopes of two rocky points were passed, where the trail was so rough that we dismounted and led the horses along with great difficulty.

When we reached the ford, a mile above camp, the river was found to be much higher than when we forded it before. We ventured into it, however, and although the current almost swept the horses off their feet, and sometimes reached halfway up their sides, with the combined weight of ourselves and the packs on their backs, they managed to keep their footing and carried us safely across. The river at this point is about a hundred yards wide, and a large creek empties into it from the east, which has formed a flat of several acres near its mouth. The trail crosses the flat and follows the creek. Occasionally it was necessary to climb over high ledges that projected into the creek, jump fallen trees, and force our way through thickets of fir and pine. In three-quarters of an hour we reached a point a mile and a half from the river and half a mile from the springs, where we decided to camp. A suitable spot near plenty of firewood was selected. The horses were then unsaddled, and the "stuff" placed under leaning cedars, where it would remain dry until a shelter was built. While Abe took the horses back to the flat on the river and picketed them in good bunch-grass, Will propped up a small pole horizontally, about five feet above the ground and as far ahead of and parallel to a large log lying on the ground. Limbs and saplings long enough to span across were then placed at intervals, their ends resting on the pole and log. Smaller limbs were then spread on crosswise, and the whole covered thickly with small branches and needles of fir and pine. A sloping roof was thus built, which shed a slow rain very satisfactorily.

When Abe returned, the shelter was almost finished, requiring only a few more fir-needles for the roof, to complete it. A hasty glance was taken to note the dry timber. The blankets and provisions were placed under the shelter, the guns and ammunition inspected, and everything being found in good condition, we continued on foot up the trail. Directly we came to a small warm spring, which discharges its water in three or four separate streams, issuing from the face of a boulder forty feet high. The steam rose in a column high in the air. Following the trail, we passed over the boulder near its face and in close proximity to the steam. A quarter of a mile farther on, just before getting in sight of the first of the larger springs, the trail makes a steep descent through a thicket of fir and pine saplings. Our acrobatic accomplishments were here brought into requisition, for had we walked down in the usual way the game, if any, at the spring would have seen our feet before we could even have seen out of the thicket.

"You go ahead," said Will, Abe not yet having had a shot at an elk.

"All right," said Abe, and disregarding the wet and the mud, Abe got down on all-fours, with his head close to the ground, and gradually crept down toward the opening at the foot of the descent. He took fully two minutes to go the last twenty feet, but on reaching the bottom, he beckoned Will to follow, as there was nothing in the lick.

After leaving the thicket, the trail passes through a small glade or opening in the timber, about two acres in area. This opening slopes gradually toward the creek, which forms its right-hand edge or boundary. In the

CHAPTER VII. A HUNT AT THE UPPER WARM SPRINGS

centre of the opening, issuing from beneath a bunch of boulders, is the main spring, which, with other smaller springs, spreads its waters over an acre or so of stones and pebbles between the source of the springs and the creek, coating them with a white saline deposit, which attracts the game and forms the lick. The remainder of the opening is covered with a luxuriant growth of grass. At all times, and especially in cold weather, the steam from the spring rises in great clouds, although the water is not so hot but that one can easily retain the hand in it.

A dense grove of white cedars, firs, and pines, one hundred and fifty yards in width, separates these springs from several other large springs higher up the creek, which are similarly located in an opening several acres in extent.

By the time the grove was reached it was four o'clock, and it was decided Abe should take the upper lick and Will the lower one. The wind moving toward the grove across the upper lick, Abe took his stand on the leeward side in the deep shade of the grove behind two fir trees, cocked his gun, and kept a sharp lookout, while Will took a similar position near the lick below.

Save for the roaring of the creek, everything remained quiet and motionless. Finally darkness came on. Abe was just beginning to think of going back to Will and then returning to camp, as he could no longer see the sights of his gun. Suddenly a twig snapped directly behind him, and Abe turned his head, thinking Will had come over to see if he was ready to return to camp. Seeing nothing, however, in the dense gloom, Abe imagined the alarm to have been caused by some natural means, and gave his whole attention to the lick again.

Imagine his surprise when, about three minutes later, he was startled by an angry snort and a savage growl behind him. Abe's first instinct was, of course, to shoot, and wheeling around he saw a large grizzly bear ["silver-tip"] within fifteen feet of him, just entering the lick. His gun was pointed at the bear and his finger was pressing the trigger, when he observed two cubs following the bear. Discretion instantaneously arrested the pressure on the trigger. After the bear got into the lick and was, at least, twenty yards distant, Abe fired two shots at her, aiming roughly along his gun-barrel. Both shots missed. Abe then ran out into the open lick, where it was lighter, and fired a third shot just as the bear was about to enter the forest on the other side of the lick. At the report, the bear raised on its haunches, turned back toward Abe, and pawed the air frantically. Now was his chance. Abe aimed as carefully as he could over the top of the barrel, but the gun snapped. There were only three cartridges in the magazine. Before he could reload, the bear and cubs had disappeared in the woods on the opposite side of the lick. Just then Will came running up, all out of breath.

"What are you shooting at?" he asked.

Abe was so badly disappointed and disgusted that he failed to answer him at once. Finally he said:

"Just think! A grizzly and two cubs! They came up behind me, passed within fifteen feet of me, crossed the lick, and, by thunder, got away from me! If it had been fifteen minutes earlier, I could have seen my sights and I'd have had the whole crowd. Why, the cubs would have weighed a hundred pounds apiece!"

"Which way did they go?" asked Will, anxiously.

CHAPTER VII. A HUNT AT THE UPPER WARM SPRINGS

"Right out here – but look where the old one tore up the earth at the third shot!" said Abe, pointing to the tracks where the bear was when he wounded her.

"You hit her then. Is there no blood on the trail? What's the matter with following?" asked Will.

"It's too dark to see blood," said Abe; "and besides, it's dangerous to follow at night. We'll have to wait until morning."

Abe then took Will to the stand he had occupied and told him all the details, concluding with:

"What I can't understand is why the bear should approach me when the wind blew from me directly toward her – so she must have scented me all the while."

"She was probably looking for a meal for the cubs," said Will. "They must have crossed the creek, too."

"Well, I'll admit it was a 'startler,' for I wasn't looking for game from that quarter; but I'm glad I did not shoot when I first saw her."

Both Will and Abe were almost sick from disappointment, and deplored the hard luck all the way back to camp.

It was now quite dark and the rain began to fall faster. Arriving at the shelter, with a little pitch pine, a fire was soon going. Will had brought up water from the creek, and while that was boiling the steak was fried in the lid of the bucket, and some fried potatoes warmed up in a plate. In twenty minutes we had excellent coffee, and in twenty more had partaken of a very satisfactory meal.

We then pulled down some dry stubs, near at hand, which, with some fallen limbs, furnished firewood for the night. Taking turns, we each kept up the fire half the night, and managed to pass it quite comfortably.

The next morning we had breakfast and were on our stands at the licks before daylight. Nothing appearing by eight o'clock, Will went over to Abe, and the search for the bear and cubs was immediately begun. Crossing the lick, the tracks in the soft mud and pebbles were very plain, but on entering the woods it was found that the rain during the night had washed away every trace of the retreating bears. We then decided to follow up the creek-bottom some distance, in a sort of general search, keeping about fifty yards apart. We had proceeded only a few hundred yards when Will fired two shots in rapid succession. Abe was at his side in a moment.

"What is it?" asked Abe, as Will fired two more shots.

"Shoot, shoot!" said Will, pointing ahead.

Abe looked in the direction indicated, and saw a bull elk staggering about, fatally wounded. Abe fired a shot in its shoulder and another in the neck, when it dropped.

"I thought you had located bear when you began to shoot," said Abe, half disappointed, as they ran up through the brush and fallen timber to the elk.

"It's singular we should stumble on an elk here. But hasn't he got beautiful slim horns? I never saw exactly such a set before."

The antlers were remarkably slim and long, with three prongs.

"Well, we can say we killed this one together," said Will, as he prepared to remove the entrails. The elk was considerably shot to pieces by six bullets, and this was a disagreeable job, but was over in fifteen minutes. Owing to its

CHAPTER VII. A HUNT AT THE UPPER WARM SPRINGS

weight, it was with no little difficulty that the carcass was rolled over a log and propped up in an upright position. The search up the bottom for the bears was then resumed, but seeing no trace of them, we returned to the lick by noon and thence to camp. Abe went for the horses while Will gathered up the things in camp. On our return to the main camp, Spencer said it was too late to go back for the meat and scalp that day, so on the day following Abe accompanied him. He took the two bear dogs, thinking that if the bears had remained in the vicinity he might find them. But when they returned in the afternoon, Abe reported no bear, but a very interesting time fording the river on horseback, carrying the two dogs with one hand and holding the reins and guiding the horse with the other.

CHAPTER VIII.

SNOWED IN

AFTER we had been in camp nearly a week a swelling in Colgate's hands was observed, while that on his feet and legs had increased. These swellings caused considerable alarm, and Will, taking him aside, questioned him very closely about the new trouble. Colgate insisted that he would be all right in a little while; but Will, knowing that he was accustomed to hardship and exposure, rightly attributed the cause of his ailment to something more than fatigue. After being importuned, Colgate at last revealed the true cause of his disability, admitting that he was suffering from a trouble* with which he had been afflicted for a number of years; that he had been compelled to use instruments for a long time in performing the functions of nature, which he had failed to bring* with him. Will, much surprised, then asked him why he had not brought the instruments, to which he replied that he did not like to use them, and thought he could do without them. From the

---

* See Chapter XIII., p. 137.

CHAPTER VIII. SNOWED IN

nature of the complaint, it was evident that Colgate must have known that he did not have his instruments the very first day out from Kendrick; and yet he had persistently journeyed for eight successive days, deeper and deeper into the woods, without acquainting any one with the fact, and knowing at the same time that the instruments were indispensable to him. Will was dumfounded. When the facts were made known to the others, all realized the serious predicament in which they were placed. What was to be done? It did not seem advisable to start him back in the rain, which was probably snow in the mountains, so it was decided to make him as comfortable as possible in camp and await fair weather. Exercise had, apparently, a bad effect on him, and we persuaded him to relinquish his duties and remain quiet, as we wished him to start out as strong as possible on the return trip. About this time, Oc-tober 2d, Spencer expressed fears that we might be snowed in, but no one deemed the danger from that source sufficiently serious to devote a day in climbing to the top of the burnt ridge to investigate the matter. The rain still continued. Colgate grew worse daily. By October 6th his legs had swollen to nearly twice their natural size, and he was barely able to move about camp without assistance. Spencer began to urge our return, and John, who did not care to hunt in the rain, vigorously seconded the motion. Abe insisted that Indian Summer and milder weather must yet come before winter would set in, and that the return in the rain and snow would be undertaken under the very worst conditions for Colgate.

It was the intention to send Colgate back with the guide as soon as the weather became favorable; but when

IN THE HEART OF THE BITTER-ROOT MOUNTAINS:
The Story of "the Carlin Hunting Party"

Spencer and John urged the return of the whole party so persistently, "Will and Abe, who had not yet had enough hunting to satisfy them, suggested that Spencer and John return at once with Colgate, and that they would follow later, after they would have several days' more shooting.

This arrangement did not, however, meet with approval, Colgate himself preferring to remain until more trophies were secured and all return together, especially as the prospect of travelling in a snowstorm was not encouraging. This state of affairs lasted only a day or two. Finding we could wait no longer for clear weather, and Colgate's condition becoming daily more and more serious, it was finally decided to leave for Kendrick the following day, October 9th, rain or shine. It snowed all that day, and the morning was well advanced before the horses were found and brought in. The return trip was therefore postponed until the next day, when we would endeavor to make an early start.

On the morning of October 10th, all arose early and breakfasted before daylight, but it was ten o'clock before all the horses were packed and the train ready to start. The snow was six inches deep at our camp. Bidding Old Jerry and Ben good-by, we started across the flat toward the foot of the ridge. Taking the trail, with Spencer in the lead and Colgate riding the surest-footed animal we had, we laboriously made our way up the steep ascent in the soft snow and mud. Gradually, as we neared the top of the first ridge, the snow got deeper and deeper. As we turned the brow of the ridge and followed along the side of the first roundtop, the snow was about sixteen inches deep. Following the crest of the ridge, still ascending toward

CHAPTER VIII. SNOWED IN

the Lo-Lo trail, the snow deepened rapidly. We, however, pushed on until the depth of the snow got to be three feet, and the horses could make their way through it only with the greatest difficulty. It was about noon, and calling a halt, the situation was discussed in detail while we ate our lunch. Spencer said: "The snow on the Lo-Lo trail will be at least four feet deep at the post-offices. The horses can't last more than two or three days without food, and when they play out we will have to leave our stuff and walk, carrying enough grub on our backs to see us out."

What would become of Colgate? He could not walk, and in the soft snow, even if we could make rude snowshoes, it would be impossible to carry him. The trail led along steep hillsides, often overgrown for great distances with thick brush and obstructed with thousands of boulders and fallen trees. If we should attempt to pull or drag him after us under these conditions, even if there should be a crust on the snow, our progress would be necessarily so slow that several weeks would be consumed in the journey. The remaining provisions would last eight days. To continue on that route, with so meagre a supply of food and the game uncertain, involved almost certain starvation for the entire party or the eventual abandonment of Colgate to save our own lives. While the ablebodied members of the party felt confident they could make their way to the Mussel-Shell Creek (a point of safety) on rude snowshoes, they thought it would not be right to abandon Colgate until every possible means had been tried to save him. Then we thought of the river, but no one knew much about it. Spencer told us that, with the exception of two engineering corns which had passed up the river in the summer years ago, he knew of no one who had ever travelled along the river route, and expressed doubt that we would be able to take canoes or rafts safely down the river. He said, too, that there was a bad canyon somewhere below, through which it was said to be dangerous to navigate small craft and impossible to pass on horseback or on foot, and gave as his opinion that the safest and best route would be to return by trail.

As the return by trail involved the almost certain abandonment of Colgate in the snow, should he survive the cold and exposure, it became a question whether we should attempt to return by the Lo-Lo trail, relying for subsistence on the meagre chances of securing game, and hope, by good fortune, to succeed eventually in getting out, or to assume greater risks for our own lives, and adopt the river route, which offered perhaps the most favorable prospect of getting Colgate out of the mountains.

While Spencer went ahead a quarter of a mile, to make a further examination of the trail, John went to the rear to Colgate, and Will and Abe held a separate consultation. It would take several weeks to build the rafts and make our way down the river. Our relatives and friends would be subjected to the greatest anxiety and fears for our safety if we did not return at the appointed time. We knew searching and relief parties would be sent out at great expense, and that in hazarding a trip down an unknown river we were taking desperate chances with our lives; but on the river there was little or no snow, and since it offered the most feasible means of getting Colgate out, we considered it our duty to forego all other considerations and attempt a passage down the river. This alternative was, of course, only possible, provided arrangements could be made with

CHAPTER VIII. SNOWED IN

one of the two men in the cabin near our recent camp for some of their provisions. When Spencer returned, the possibility of making some such arrangement was discussed, and he, knowing the prospector quite well, assured us that if the other man – Keeley – would not sell his provisions, he thought "Old Jerry" would.

As the leader of the party, Will then gave the order to turn back. By some strange premonition or instinct, the horses positively refused to turn around, and when compelled to do so, frequently left the trail and attempted to get by us and continue the other way. We, however, succeeded in getting them started back after fifteen minutes of hard work in the snow.

We arrived at our camp about four o'clock in the afternoon. A little snow had fallen in the meantime, but this was soon cleared away and the tents pitched on the same ground they had previously occupied. As soon as the horses were unsaddled, they were turned loose and allowed to roam again over the flat and the ridge above it. The day's journey had a bad effect on poor Colgate, who was almost exhausted on our arrival. That same night Will arranged with Ben Keeley, the trapper, for the sum of $250, to sell us his share of the "grub" in the cabin, help build our rafts, and accompany us down the river. Keeley was an excellent chopper, and had considerable experience in rafting sawlogs in Minnesota and Wisconsin.

*The scenery from the top of the ridge before making the final descent to camp was magnificent, and included the two views in opposite directions reproduced at the beginning of this volume. waters. He was, in consequence, a very valuable acquisition to our party in the emergency.

JERRY JOHNSON'S CABIN.

Our proposed trip down the river involved a number of changes in our plans, and necessitated the leaving of our horses, saddles, and such other articles of our camp equipage as could be of no further service to us.

"Old Jerry's" cabin was not quite completed, and as we wished to leave our superfluous things with him during the winter, we thought it would be best to help him finish it, or at least get it under roof before we left. Fresh meat was needed in order to prosecute with vigor the work on the cabin, as well as on the rafts later. Ben and Spencer being the best choppers, they were accordingly delegated to assist Jerry with the cabin, while Will, Abe, and John hunted.

The deep snows on the mountains and the recent stormy weather had driven the elk and deer down into

CHAPTER VIII. SNOWED IN

the valleys and river bottoms. The day after our return it cleared off, and the bright sunlight, the first we had seen since the 26th of September, was most acceptable and cheering.

The snow disappeared on the banks of the river, life in camp became cheerful and pleasant, and game being abundant, an ample supply of fresh meat was readily secured. In four days the roof of Jerry's cabin was finished; and with the exception of one day, during which it rained, the weather was exceptionally fine.

CHAPTER IX.

A HUNT AT THE LOWER WARM SPRINGS

THE programme for the following morning was a hunt at the lower lick. On retiring that night, in order to get as early a start as possible, it was agreed that the first one who awakened in the morning should call the others.

"Abe! Hello, Abe! What time is it?" asked Will – Abe and John having the only running watches in the camp at that time.

In a minute there was a flash of light as Abe struck a match.

"Pshaw, it's only quarter-past twelve!" said Abe, disgustedly, as he rolled over in his blankets.

Two hours later Abe awoke and struck another match. It was still too early. Will was the first to wake after that, and it was then daylight. He jumped up quickly, calling Abe and John. It was still raining, the dull pounding of the drops on the tent being anything but encouraging for a prospective hunt. John said he was not feeling well, and did not wish to go that morning. So Abe and Will,

CHAPTER IX. A HUNT AT THE LOWER WARM SPRINGS

after hastily eating a sandwich, started off at a brisk pace down the trail.

"Will this rain ever stop?" asked Abe impatiently, as he thrust aside the dripping branches of a young fir tree which projected into the trail, thereby causing a miniature shower under it.

"It must be the rainy season," said Will.

"Well, I'm sick of it. I never hunted so hard before in all my life in such weather; but as we can't stay much longer and I want to kill elk, it's a 'ground-hog case.'"

Several small brooks were crossed at intervals. When within a quarter of a mile of the lick, a peculiar sound – a half-whistle, half-bellow – was faintly heard.

Will stopped short and said, "Listen!"

The same sound was repeated.

"Elk!" said Will, positively.

"Are you sure?" asked Abe.

"Certain; the same sound that mine made the other day."

"Jove! we're in luck at last!" replied Abe.

As the lick was approached, we became more and more cautious. Abe was in the lead and did not move faster than ten feet a minute.

When in sight of the lick, he stopped and remained motionless a full minute. Then he turned - and whispered:

"There's something in."

Will was moving up closer, when Abe raised his hand to motion him back, whispering, "Stand still!"

Just then the cow elk (for that was what he saw when he first noted a movement through the brush and timber) walked out into the open lick, in full view, looking squarely at Abe. It is, of course, well known that when game does not scent the hunter, even if he is in plain view, the game does not become alarmed as long as the hunter remains motionless.

Abe was just stepping over a protruding limb as the elk appeared, with one leg poised in the air, and one hand extended toward Will. He was obliged to remain in that uncomfortable position for a full half-minute before the elk's suspicions were satisfied and she lowered her head to lick. Both of us then took positions behind trees near us and waited. In a moment, a second cow and a calf entered the lick, followed by a third cow. After the lapse of a minute the bull appeared over the brow of the hill, entered the lick, and, passing along the edge of it, entered the woods, standing in such a position that his head and the forward part of his body were concealed behind some trees. He remained in this position for some time, while the balance of the herd were patronizing the lick. We were getting impatient.

"Shoot!" said Will, as the calf came out of the lick and walked to the side of the bull. "They are moving off now."

Just then the bull stepped forward far enough to enable Abe to see his shoulder.

Bang! went his gun; and a second later, bang! bang! went Will's double-barrel.

In a single bound, the bull was out of sight over the brow of the hill, with Abe in swift pursuit.

At the report of the guns the balance of the herd became alarmed and started to run across a cedar flat adjacent to the lick and about a hundred feet above the river bottom.

Will had selected a young cow, as the camp was in need of meat, and gave her two shots as she was making off. He failed to stop her, however, and also started in pursuit.

CHAPTER IX. A HUNT AT THE LOWER WARM SPRINGS

The tracks of the bull were easy to follow, as he took terrific leaps down the hill, ploughing great furrows in the ground at every jump. On reaching the bottom, however, he turned sharply to the right and followed a game-trail at the base of the hill. By his tracks, Abe soon saw that his pace was slackening, and from the blood which could be seen along the trail it was evident the bull was badly wounded.

Going along cautiously, Abe finally saw the bull standing perfectly still in the trail, about seventyfive yards ahead of him. Taking careful aim he pulled the trigger, but his gun snapped. Working the lever which operated the magazine, without taking his eye off of the elk, the gun snapped again. A hasty examination showed that the gun was disabled, returning the empty shell into the barrel instead of ejecting it. Hastily inserting a new cartridge in the barrel, Abe was nearly ready to shoot, when bang! bang! went Will's doublebarrel in the flat above, and with two bounds the bull was out of sight.

We will not attempt to reproduce what Abe said just then, but he followed the tracks to a small ravine, where they turned abruptly down to the river. Halting for a moment here, Abe examined the shore of the river ahead, and spied the bull standing in the river near the shore, facing the opposite side of the river.

The blood could be seen oozing from a wound through the lungs, back of the shoulder and just above the heart.

Abe had reached a little rocky point about forty feet above the river and about seventy yards from where the elk was standing. Here was an interesting problem. If Abe shot the elk again while facing the opposite shore, even if he broke his shoulders, the elk might have sufficient vitality to struggle into the deep water and be washed down the river. With his left elbow resting on his knee, Abe covered the elk with his gun and waited. In a few minutes the bull lay down in the river, nothing but his head showing above the surface of the water.

Suddenly the report of Will's gun rang out again, and with a start the bull sprang up and took several jumps toward the opposite shore, but soon stopped, facing downstream. A moment later he faced the near shore, and Abe, thinking a shot through the heart might cause him to spring out of the river to the shore, fired again.

On the contrary, however, the bull turned and made for the opposite shore. When nearly across, he began to stagger and wave his beautiful antlers from side to side. Fearing he would expire in the river and be washed down, Abe fired a shot into the rear portion of his body, hoping the effect might be to cause the bull to make for the opposite shore; but the scheme did not succeed. Standing in the swift, roaring stream up to his knees, savagely trampling the rocky bottom of the river in his endeavor to maintain equilibrium, his magnificent head poised gracefully in the air, while above him, mute witnesses of his sad distress, towered his native mountains, – the dying elk and the surroundings formed a picture such as brush and pigment can never hope to reproduce.

At last the rear portion of his body fell over sidewise, carrying the front part with it. With a violent effort, the elk stood erect, only to fall again. Then lying in the water, he continued to fight the encroachments of death, the swift current and his struggles carrying him down the river; but his struggles became more and more feeble,

CHAPTER IX. A HUNT AT THE LOWER WARM SPRINGS

and finally ceased altogether, when the carcass lodged against a rock in the river.

"Hello, old 'stuff'! I hear you've killed the prize bull elk," said Will, delightedly, as he appeared over the edge of the bank above, having heard Abe's last shot and seen the elk lodged against the rock near the other shore.

"Hurry up! Let's get him out before he washes down the river," continued Will.

"Hold on, Will! Don't you wade out into that cold water," said Abe; but Will had already removed his trousers and started in. He soon got over to the elk, and then motioned Abe not to follow.

He made the elk secure by piling some stones back of it, and bending the neck so that the horns acted as a prop. Will then forded to the opposite side, to exercise his legs and restore the circulation of the blood, as the cold water had numbed them. Selecting a pole with which to steady himself, he recrossed the river.

"Did you get yours too?" asked Abe, referring to the elk Will was after.

"You bet!" said Will. "We'll go right over to it."

In a few minutes Will was ready, and both walked back to the lick.

They found the elk lying head downward on a steep hill-side. She was young and very fat, so good meat was assured. The elk, after being shot by Will at the lick, had gone around in a semicircular course, and after receiving five shots while running, had fallen dead within twenty yards of the lick.

When Will and Abe returned to camp, they found Spencer, Ben Keeley, and Jerry Johnson just on the eve of starting down the river with five pack-horses, to bring in a lot of shakes that Keeley had made to roof the cabin. Consequently, no time was lost in getting up the horses to pack in the meat, horns, and scalp.

The shakes were on the trail to the lick, about a mile and a half distant from camp. Will, being wet and somewhat chilled, donned some dry clothes, while Abe accompanied the train down the trail. When the shakes were reached, Spencer assisted Jerry to "pack" the animals, while Keeley and Abe passed on to the lick, riding two of the horses.

Two young cow elk and a calf were surprised in the lick, one of which Abe shot, mistaking it, on account of its under size, for a deer. Keeley immediately bled it, and had just finished the work of removing the entrails when Spencer arrived on the scene. The three then continued down the river to where Abe's bull was, and descending the steep bank, tied up the horses and set about to devise some plan to get the elk ashore.

After discussing the situation in detail, Spencer said the best plan would be to ford the river to the elk on horseback, cut off the head and drag it across the river by a rope fastened to the pommel of Keeley's saddle.

The plan seemed feasible, and Keeley and Spencer started into the river, while Abe soon had a warm fire going on shore. All went very well until Spencer got near the carcass of the elk, when the horse he was riding snorted aud refused to proceed farther. The horse was finally prevailed upon to approach near enough to allow Spencer to jump off on the carcass of the elk. Keeley then took both horses to the opposite shore and held them while Spencer cut off the elk's head with a hatchet.

CHAPTER IX. A HUNT AT THE LOWER WARM SPRINGS

When this was done, Keeley brought back the horses to Spencer, who gave him a rope, one end of which was tied to the elk's horns. Keeley fastened the other end to his saddle and started across the river, dragging the head through the swift water. In a short time he reached the shore, followed by Spencer.

The head was then carried to the fire, and while Spencer removed the scalp and cleaned the skull, Abe and Keeley repaired to the lick and secured the choice portions of the two cow elk.

When Spencer came up, the horses were packed, and the meat, horns, and scalp taken into camp.

CHAPTER X.

BUILDING THE RAFTS

On the morning of October 15th, five days after our unsuccessful attempt to reach the Lo-Lo trail, Spencer and Keeley went down the river to look for suitable timber for the rafts. Will was laid up in camp with a bad boil on the ankle of his right foot, and Abe had a sore neck from a wrench he had received while out hunting a few days before. Colgate grew gradually worse. The weather at this time remained clear and warm. The snow was rapidly disappearing on the hill-sides adjacent to the river, and notwithstanding the temporary ailments from which some of us were suffering, we were all cheerful and hopeful.

In the afternoon Abe went down the river to see what success Spencer and Keeley had met with in their search for timber. He found them near the lower warm springs, where a bunch of dead white cedars, of suitable size, had been located, some of which had already been felled and peeled. Abe took a block of the wood, and after ascertaining its specific gravity by the use of a small fish-scales belonging to Will, he calculated the number of cubic feet

CHAPTER X. BUILDING THE RAFTS

each of the two rafts should contain in order to carry their respective loads. The object was to avoid unnecessary and superfluous weight, which would make the rafts more difficult to handle in the swift water.

That night quite a debate was indulged in concerning the rafts. Abe and Will insisted that a long, narrow raft was the only form that could possibly pass through the numerous projecting boulders in the river, while Keeley and Spencer were equally sure that a wider raft of less length was best. Keeley and Spencer were, however, won over, and the dimensions of the rafts were finally fixed at four and a half to five feet wide and twenty-six feet long.

In order to avoid the long walk back and forth from where the rafts were being built, a camp was established near them the following day, and Keeley and Spencer moved down. Will being still unable to walk on his sore foot and remaining in bed, we were compelled for a time to maintain two camps. Colgate required considerable nursing, and fires had to be kept going for his comfort. John and Abe were consequently kept busy most of the time cooking and getting in necessary firewood. Every afternoon, however, Abe would go down to the other camp and help for several hours on the rafts, carrying such additional provisions as the other camp required along with him. About this time myriads of snow-geese passed over us daily as they migrated southward.

One afternoon, as Abe was going down to the other camp, just as he was crossing a little ravine, he noted a movement through the brush in the bottom, to his left. Standing still, he waited a moment and then saw the head of a deer, and soon afterward the deer, moving up the ra-

IN THE HEART OF THE BITTER-ROOT MOUNTAINS:
The Story of "the Carlin Hunting Party"

vine toward the trail. Watching his opportunity, as the deer disappeared back of some bushes, Abe sat down in the trail. When the deer struck the trail, it turned toward Abe; and as it approached, and less brush intervened between them, Abe saw that it was a black-tail doe, preceded by a fawn. The wind was moving from them toward Abe, so they could not scent him. On they came, nearer and nearer, the graceful antics of the fawn as it moved its head up and down and from side to side, intently watching and listening, was greatly admired and enjoyed by Abe. At last, when within fifty feet of him, both fawn and doe became suspicious and stopped. Abe sat perfectly motionless, with his gun pointed at them, and did not even blink his eyes. A gentle breeze from the opposite direction enabled them to scent him, and at the same instant the fawn made a phenomenal leap to the right of the trail, while the doe turned squarely about and darted down the trail like an arrow. Through the opening in the timber Abe could catch glimpses of the fawn as it circled about to join the doe far down the river.

The building of the rafts was no small undertaking. The river was full of boulders, and the shores were a mass of jagged rocks. The heavy rafts in the swift water could not be so completely controlled that they would not strike the boulders and ledges occasionally, and for that reason had to be built very strong and firm. Having no spikes or bolts, we had to resort to framing and dovetailing methods in their construction.

On account of its lightness, dead cedar was selected as the best timber available for the purpose. Straight trees, sixteen to twenty inches in diameter, were chosen, felled, and peeled. As the horses could not be utilized on account of the rough ground, fallen timber, and want of

CHAPTER X. BUILDING THE RAFTS

suitable harness, the work of collecting the logs on the river bank was a difficult job and involved some heavy lifting. With skids, rollers, and handspikes, we moved the logs of the first raft in one day to the river bank and placed them side by side on top of two cross-logs.

With the aid of a wooden square and a scribingawl, made by Abe, the logs were marked and the work of fastening them together begun. Our tools consisted of two axes, two batchets, a broken cross-cut saw and an inch auger, the last two belonging to Jerry Johnson, and having been borrowed of him.

Dovetails were sawed in each of the logs opposite each other at both ends and in the middle. Crosspieces of green fir were "dressed out" to fit into the dovetails loosely; and then, with thin wedges split from cedar, the logs were wedged tightly to the cross-pieces. The ends of the cross-pieces were also wedged, to prevent the logs from spreading apart. To still further strengthen the rafts, vertical keys, four inches square, were set in the joints between the logs, the mortises extending half way into each log. Cedar poles, three to four inches in diameter, were then pinned down around the outside edge, forming a sort of railing. As Spencer and Keeley expected to man this raft, the lesser details of construction were left to their own choice. They made a framework capable of supporting the provisions, etc., six to eight inches above the top of the raft in its middle portion; a large sweep was mounted in the stern, and several upright posts were framed into the raft at convenient places. On October 22d the first raft was ready to launch, and was named the "Clearwater." The same day the upper camp was abandoned. Some of the things were left in a small tent and subsequently taken over to Jerry's cabin, and the rest were "packed" on horses to where the rafts were building.

The work was then prosecuted with greater vigor. Abe, Keeley and Spencer worked regularly on the rafts, while Will did the cooking and cared for Colgate. John assisted Will, and occasionally went over and helped on the raft.

AT THE LOWER WARM SPRINGS.

The dimensions of the second raft were the same as the first, but larger timber was used, and the logs were hewed on two sides. Instead of a framework, a sort of a box, with a raised floor, was built in the middle of the raft, in which the provisions, etc., could be more conveniently carried. The second raft was completed about October 29th. No suitable name for this raft suggested itself at that time, but during the voyage down the river the second raft, to distinguish

CHAPTER X. BUILDING THE RAFTS

it from the other, soon came to be known as the "Carlin."

While the rafts were building we kept a sharp lookout on the trail. Spencer made two examinations, which necessitated the laborious climbing of the high ridge and a "hard pull" through the snow each time. The first of these was made on October 18th. After reaching the top of the ridge he found the snow was thawing on the hillsides having southern exposures, but it remained intact on the north hill-sides. A stiff crust had formed on the snow, and travelling for horses was very difficult. A very curious fact which Spencer noted as he journeyed on, was that some of the horses had passed over the trail recently. When he reached the point where we had stopped and turned back eight days before, he was surprised to find that some of the horses had been there. By the tracks and the area they had pawed over in their search for food, he could see that they had spent two nights in the snow, after which some of them had again returned to the river bottom, while others had gone down into a deep gulch to one side of the trail. The horses evidently had made an unsuccessful attempt to get out of the woods. Spencer pressed on a half-mile farther with great difficulty, and finding the snow was getting deeper, returned to camp and reported the trail in worse shape than when we had made the attempt to get out, with the snow probably six feet deep on the Lo-Lo trail.

A curious incident of this trip of Spencer's was the finding of a gold watch-charm, which had been lost by one of the members of the party, in a mass of rocks which the trail crossed. The rocks were so located that the sun's rays fell vertically upon them and thawed the snow so as to allow the lost watch-charm to be seen.

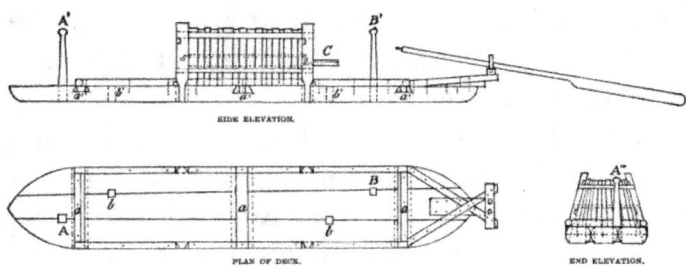

THE "CARLIN" RAFT.

The last examination of the trail was made by Spencer, just before starting down the river on the rafts, on October 30th. The snow had apparently thawed considerably since his previous examination, and all hoped that we might yet be able to take Colgate out over the Lo-Lo trail. On his return, however, Spencer informed us that while the snow had disappeared low down in the river bottoms, it had really increased in depth on the high ridges, and that it would be utterly impossible to take horses out over the trail.

We were out of fresh meat, as we had abandoned hunting and gave our whole attention to the rafts after October 22d. Will had, however, succeeded in catching a few fish nearly every day, which were very palatable in the absence of meat.

The same day that Spencer went to examine the trail the last time, Abe went hunting, leaving the camp at daylight. He was very fortunate in finding a young cow elk about four miles up the river, which he shot, bringing the heart and a piece of the sirloin with him to camp that evening. The next day he and Spencer started out with two horses and brought in the meat.

CHAPTER X. BUILDING THE RAFTS

The same day, October 31st, Abe and Will went to Jerry's cabin and selected so much of Keeley's provisions as they thought sufficient for the trip down the river, leaving the remainder with Jerry. We expected to make the passage down the river in about a week, and although Jerry assured us it would not take more than four days, about fifteen days' provisions were taken as a safeguard. We had been out of sugar and milk for some time, and were therefore anxious to buy some of Jerry's, as we had already used all of Keeley's sugar. Jerry, however, refused to part with any of his, saying he had little enough for himself. Abe offered him his entire fishing outfit, valued at $22, for two pounds of sugar, which Jerry refused. Will then offered him a 45-90-300 Winchester single-shot rifle (which he had bought from Keeley), a lot of ammunition, and a lot of fishing hooks and tackle, for three pounds of sugar, which was accepted. They then presented Jerry with all their horses, and asked him to care for them during the winter and try and save them, if possible, from starvation. The following day Will brought the provisions down to camp.

After October 22d, when we moved Colgate to the lower camp, he failed rapidly. Liquid had collected in his lungs, which choked or smothered him when he assumed a horizontal position, and he was, consequently, unable to lie down. Spencer made him a chair out of a block of wood, upon which he sat day and night. His legs were swollen to an enormous size; and although a small man when well, he then weighed fully two hundred pounds. He was perfectly helpless, and had to be assisted when he wished to move the smallest distance about camp. He was very sensitive to cold, and we constantly kept blankets around him. We were, besides, compelled to divide the night into watches and sit up with him, maintaining fires all night long for his comfort. Scarcely an hour passed that he did not require assistance, but notwithstanding the most careful nursing and attention to his requirements, he grew steadily worse. On the 2d of November the swelling on one of his legs broke. Considerable liquid was discharged, after which he felt somewhat relieved.

Knowing that we could return over the trail on snowshoes if disencumbered by Colgate, someone suggested that Jerry Johnson should take care of Colgate until we could return to Kendrick, when a relief party could be sent after Colgate, with additional supplies for Johnson. "Old Jerry" refused to agree to this, however, on account of the uncertainty of a relief party being able to reach him at that season, and asserted that the remaining provisions were barely sufficient for himself during the winter. Colgate was, besides, afraid of Johnson, and was unwilling to stay with him.

Colgate's rapidly sinking condition argued strongly against such a course. It was doubtful if he could survive the journey out, and it was almost certain that he could not live until rescued by a relief party, even if such a party was to start back for him immediately after our return to civilization. The only humane course left us, therefore, was to attempt a passage down the river, and restore Colgate to his family before his dissolution, if possible.

On the morning of November 2d the river was running full of broken ice, but it passed off during the day. Will walked down the river several miles to examine the rapids. On his return he reported two large ones, one of which

CHAPTER X. BUILDING THE RAFTS

he considered quite dangerous, and said that the only open channel through it was on the left-hand side. The final arrangements for the trip down the river kept everybody in camp busy. The rafts were launched and a number of poles prepared for guiding them. Abe filed the saw for Old Jerry. John sewed up two sacks of flour in waterproof canvas to prevent them from getting wet. Will made himself a shirt and mittens out of a blanket, the weather being very cold. John also made himself a similar pair of mittens and a hood, but subsequently gave the latter to Colgate.

Everything being in readiness on the night of November 2d, it was decided to start the following morning as early as possible.

The journey down the river was undertaken with a full sense of its probable hardships and dangers. We feared it, because we reasoned that were it a practicable and easy route, such as ordinary water-courses are, many hunters and prospectors would have preferred to travel up and down the river in canoes rather than go around by way of the Lo-Lo trail, with a more expensive outfit. Since no one, except engineering corps in 1881 and 1886, had ever been known to pass through the canyon (which was said to be somewhere below on the river), and then in the summer when the water was low, we feared we would find dangerous and perhaps impassable places in the river on account of the high water at this season. So serious an undertaking did Will and Abe consider it that they wrote a number of letters, which they left with Jerry Johnson to mail when he would return to Missoula the following summer.

CHAPTER XI.

A REVERIE

[NOTE. – The following lines were composed one night by a member of the party, while maintaining fire's during his watch, soon after the journey down the Kooskooskee was begun.]

 A HUNDRED mountains round me rear
  Their hoary heads on high,
And join in admiration of
  A brilliant blue sky.

A thousand stars from farthest space
  Their silver-white rays send,
Which with the moon's more mellow light
  Harmoniously blend.

Ten thousand rippling waves have caught
  Despite the river's roar –
The stars above, and, trembling, hold
  A hundred thousand more.

CHAPTER XI. A REVERIE

The rich aroma of the pines
    A dewy zephyr stirs;
And changing shadows round me play
    From yonder swaying firs.

The angler's dream is realized,
    The hunter is content;
The artist's soul, solaced, has found
    Fields boundless in extent.

O Nature kind! Thy proffered cup
    With rarest grace o'erflows;
It soothes the mind, and heals the soul.
    And priceless gifts bestows.

Beneath the over-arching trees,
    This beaut'ous night to me
Brings cherished mem'ries of the past,
    And tender thoughts of thee.

I love the awful mountains, and
    The stars that gem the sky;
The music of the roaring streams;
    The shadows flitting by;

The sweet aroma of the trees;
    The breezes fresh and free, –
But multiply my love for these
    A million times for thee.

At Night On The Kooskooskee River, Idaho. NOVEMBER 6TH, 1893.

CHAPTER XII.

THE JOURNEY DOWN THE KOOSKOOSKEE

[NOTE. – What follows in this chapter is taken almost *verbatim* from Mr. Carlin's diary.]

Friday, November 3d, 1893. – We were through breakfast shortly after daylight; packed up everything in the most convenient form, and loaded the rafts. Although we hurried as much as possible, it was eleven o'clock before we were ready to start down the river. Old Jerry came down early in the morning to see us off and take some letters which we wished to leave with him, to post to our families in the spring in case we never got out of the mountains. This morning it was cold and cloudy; it began to rain hard about the time we started. It was just 11:30 o'clock when Keeley and Spencer, who manned the lighter raft, shoved off from shore and started down the river. Our raft followed at a distance of about one hundred yards. We had easy water for the first half-mile, when we landed our raft, and John went down around the point to see if Keeley and Spencer got through the first bad rapid all right. He

CHAPTER XII. THE JOURNEY DOWN THE KOOSKOOSKEE

returned in fifteen minutes and reported that the boys had passed through safely, and had landed on the opposite bank below the rapid. We shoved off and stuck on a small rock, but got off in a few minutes. Jerry gave us a parting salute of three shots, and we waved him good-by. When we rounded the point, Spencer motioned us toward his side of the river. We entered the rapid, and just got through the narrow channel without touching the big rocks on either side. Our raft was heavier than theirs and more difficult to land, so we kept right on past them; and rounding the point two hundred yards below, we entered the second bad rapid, of which I had spoken the day before.

WHERE THE FIRST UPSET OCCURRED.

This was a difficult place to get through, as the current carried us toward the right bank at the head of the rapid, and the only open channel was along the left-hand side.

IN THE HEART OF THE BITTER-ROOT MOUNTAINS:
The Story of "the Carlin Hunting Party"

We had gotten about one-third through, when we struck two large rocks with great force. Not being able to keep the stern from swinging, we were, in a moment, sidewise to the current, jammed against the rocks. The water rushed over the raft and turned its bottom against the rocks, with its side down, and over half the raft was under water. John was thrown off the bow, but he kept hold of his pike-pole, and managed to get in shallow water and thence to the shore. Colgate was sucked under the raft, and was on the point of being swept away, when Abe caught him by the collar of his coat and pulled him on the upper side of the raft. Little Montana was drowning, but she was also pulled out high and dry. Spencer and Keeley saw our upset from above the rapid in time to run their raft ashore. They came down and tried to wade out to us, but could get only a few feet from shore without being washed off their feet. It was impossible to make them understand a word, owing to the roaring of the water, although we were only about twenty yards apart. Finally we managed to make them understand that we wanted them to tie their rope to a tree about one hundred feet above us, and let their raft down so that they could get over to us and take off our load. It took over an hour to accomplish this. Spencer attended to the rope, and Keeley guided his raft through the rocks along the shore. We sent Colgate, the dogs, and some provisions over in the first load. Abe helped Keeley to land, while I stayed on the raft and got out a second load of blankets, etc. John had worked up the river bank and found a shallow place, where he managed with great difficulty to cross to our side of the river. Colgate and he were cold from the icy water

CHAPTER XII. THE JOURNEY DOWN THE KOOSKOOSKEE

and sleet, which was falling heavily, so Spencer built them a fire. We had just transferred our second load, when our raft, relieved of its weight, rose in the water and partially righted. Abe jumped on, and we loosened it from the rocks and started down the river. We got through the rapid without any further mishap, but could not make a landing below. My pike-pole was jammed in the rocks in the river bottom and jerked out of my hands, and we were carried down for half a mile, when we managed to run fast on a bunch of small rocks in shallow water near the shore, which prevented us from being carried into the rapid below. Wading ashore, we made the raft fast to a root with a rope and "struck out" for camp. We all made as comfortable a camp as possible, "hustled" in firewood for the night, and cooked supper. It continued raining and sleeting. All in all, we had a rough sort of a day. The night was divided into watches, so that a fire could be kept up for Colgate.

Saturday, November 4th. – We decided to leave our antlers and all other unnecessary things with Jerry, and lighten our loads as much as possible.

Spencer walked up to get him to come down with horses and " pack" the things to his cabin. Keeley, Abe, and I went down to get the raft off the rocks, John remaining in camp to take care of Colgate. After two hours' hard work in the water, we got the raft off and pulled it ashore. Returning to camp, we built a rousing big fire and soon dried all our stuff. Spencer returned at three o'clock and said that Jerry would be down in the morning. We got in firewood for the night. It rained hard nearly all day. Colgate is not as well to-day as he was yesterday; I am afraid it is due to the wetting he got.

IN THE HEART OF THE BITTER-ROOT MOUNTAINS:
The Story of "the Carlin Hunting Party"

Sunday, November 5th. – We got up at daylight and packed up all the things we intended taking with us. Placing them on Spencer's raft, we carefully let it clown the rapid to where the other lay, and transferred one-half the load to our raft. Jerry came down about ten o'clock to get the things we intended leaving with him. Having helped him pack the horses, we said good-by to him again and started down the river at eleven o'clock, with Keeley and Spencer in the lead. Several pretty bad rapids were passed, and the first island was sighted about half-past eleven. Finding the right-hand channel too shallow, we were obliged to take the left-hand, which has some rather bad rocks at the end of the island. Spencer and Keeley stuck, but got off without much difficulty. By keeping more to the left, we got through without trouble, and all made a landing below the island, on the right bank. Abe went down the river to examine the rapids below. This island is merely a gravel bar, with a few pine-trees on. it. I have no doubt that in summer the right-hand channel is practically dry. A large creek comes into the river just below the island; it drains a fine flat, that I examined some days before and found full of elk and bear signs. Abe returned, and having found a landing-place below, we started again at about half-past one P.M. and made a good run until we came to a worse rapid than any we had yet seen. Spencer and Keeley tried to keep along the right-hand bank and stuck fast on a rock; they motioned us to keep to the centre. This brought us into the worst of the water, with large boulders on every side. We were going along at a tremendous rate, when two large rocks loomed up on each side of us, the water falling vertically several feet below them. Thinking it out of

CHAPTER XII. THE JOURNEY DOWN THE KOOSKOOSKEE

the question to pass them, and fully expecting an upset, I shouted to Colgate to hold fast to the posts. We were so fortunate, however, as to get exactly between them, and our raft shot over the drop into the quieter water below. Keeley afterward remarked: "I thought you fellows were goners that time, sure! We couldn't see anything of you after you took the jump.'' Making a landing below, we went up to help Spencer and Keeley; but they had jumped into the water above their waists and lifted the raft off the rock, and were leading it down along the shore.

A RAPID THAT MADE RAFTING INTERESTING.

Making another examination of the river, we found several stiff rapids – one in particular, where the river narrowed down and went through a gorge. The waves were over four feet high, but the rocks were all hidden by high water. Our raft went ahead, and we had no trouble until we came to the gorge. Here we rolled around like an ocean steamer and came very near upsetting. It's lucky the rocks were covered. The waves struck Abe, who stood in the bow, above the waist, and came near carrying him off the raft. A landing was made, to wait for the other raft, which, however, passed us and took the lead. We found no more bad places; and after going perhaps three-quarters of a mile, we saw that Spencer and Keeley had landed and were motioning us toward them. Although we worked as hard as we could, we could not quite reach the bank, and came near getting caught on some large rocks at the mouth of a creek which comes in from the right. As we passed the other raft we threw out a rope, which fell short. Spencer, however, caught a second rope, and was dragged off his feet into the water. He held on and snubbed the raft, so that we managed to land about twenty yards below them. It being about half-past three P.M., we decided to camp. It has rained hard all day, and everyone is wet. Our camp is on a damp flat, with very little dry wood. Some put up the tent and fly, others cut and carried in wood until after dark. After supper, we laid a raised floor of dry cedar under the fly, to put our provisions on, and made a big fire, to dry our blankets. We did not get to bed until after two o'clock A.M. The dogs have been excitedly sniffing the air, and, from the signs we have seen, elk must frequent the flat.

Monday, November 6th. – We got up at daylight, and after breakfast Abe and I walked down the river three miles. The walking is harder than the rafting. On the way down we saw old camps and choppings of surveyors. It has rained hard all night, and the river is very high to-day. We saw two very bad rapids, besides many minor ones. Got

CHAPTER XII. THE JOURNEY DOWN THE KOOSKOOSKEE

back to camp at twelve o'clock and found that Spencer and Keeley had made a bow oar, as the water is getting too deep in places to use poles advantageously. Started down the river, with Spencer and Keeley in the lead. We all had exceptionally good luck in missing big boulders a dozen times or more. Spencer made a landing on the second island and helped us land by the aid of a rope (our raft is heavier and harder to manage than theirs). The left-hand channel was found to be too dangerous to run, as the current makes directly against a ledge of sharp rocks, which we could not pass. The right-hand channel is still more dangerous, for the current sweeps against a large rock in the centre of the river. On the right side of it there are some six large boulders, reaching to the shore. To get by this point safely, it would have been necessary to run the rafts between the big rock and the island, which was obviously impossible in the swift current. We therefore landed on the island, and let the rafts, by ropes, down past the big rock to the foot of the island. This prevented us from examining the river beyond. We could see the waves of a very long and hard rapid below us. There was, however, no alternative but to run ahead and take the chances of finding a fall below. Spencer and Keeley went ahead. We climbed a big pile of driftwood, which the water in freshet time had piled up twenty feet high, and watched them. We saw them enter the rapid, then make a swift shoot out of sight to the right. Their disappearance was so sudden that it almost took our breath away. After a minute's anxious watching, we saw them below the rapid, mere specks in the distance, and found out afterward that they had several " close shaves." We entered the rapid in the centre. The waves were the highest we had yet seen, and we would have been upset if we had not been careful in balancing the raft. These rapids are two hundred yards long, and although the roughest water we had experienced so far, there were no rocks in sight. The river banks are perpendicular at this point, and we could not have landed if we had wished to. Below the rapid is a very deep pool over half a mile long. We found Spencer and Keeley landed on a nice, dry island covered with trees, and as it was half-past three, camp was made. On the island we found the only fresh signs of man (Indians) we had yet seen. There is a trail crossing the river at this point. Evidently the Indians camp here in summer when crossing from the Lo-Lo to the trail on the divide to the south.

We have been out four days now, and have not made much more than ten miles. Keeley is anxious *to* "turn the rafts loose" and trust to luck in running through, but the others do not consider it safe at all, as we don't know what is below us. It continues to rain hard, and we are pretty well tired out. Our things are all so wet that we have decided to remain here to-morrow. Some of us will dry the blankets, clothes, and provisions, and the rest will go down the river some distance to examine the rapids. A comfortable camp was made and a rousing big fire built. I tried fishing, but had no success, owing to high water. This island is one hundred yards long by twenty-five wide. We found some old tepee-poles and a sweat-bath. The right-hand channel is easy to ford in low water.

Tuesday, November 7th. – It was clear this morning, and we were up and through breakfast soon after daylight. Abe decided to go down the river and examine the rapids. We had much trouble in landing him, being obliged to tie

CHAPTER XII. THE JOURNEY DOWN THE KOOSKOOSKEE

the raft with a long rope, and pole and row hard for the shore. The rest of us busied ourselves around camp – some dried blankets, others provisions; Spencer made a bow oar for us. Abe did not get in until dark, very tired and hungry, having had no food but a small piece of bread since morning.

He had walked eight miles down the river, and reported the first five miles fair going, but the last three a continuous rapid of very swift water, owing to the exceptional fall of the river-bed. He thinks we cannot run these rapids at all, and will have to let the rafts down by ropes all the way.

Wednesday, November 8th. – We made an exceptionally early start this morning, and made five miles in a very short time, with three stops. The runs were exciting, but not dangerous. On the way down Abe called my attention to a pile of rocks on a high bluff, which he had observed the preceding day and named "Monk's Point," owing to their wonderful likeness to the figure of a hooded monk seated on a rock, with his head bent down, as in thought. We landed at two large eddies, from which we could see the river below take a sudden shoot down, like a mill-race. We passed a beautiful creek, which empties into the river from the left in a succession of miniature falls. John went with Keeley and Spencer to-day.

Four of us went down to examine Abe's bad rapids, and John stayed with the rafts. We found by far the worst rapids we had yet seen. The current was extremely swift for a mile, and the river full of boulders. Then the river narrowed, and in the centre was a very large rock, which left narrow channels on each side, and these were full of rocks. Below it was still worse – more boulders and worse water. It was clear that we would upset a good many times before getting through this rapid if we were to try to run it; and should we fail to make a landing, we would be carried into a row of rocks that would smash us up completely. We cannot lower the rafts by ropes from the righthand shore, owing to perpendicular banks in many places. It would be unsafe to leave Colgate on the raft while passing through the worst places, and the righthand bank is so steep and rough that he cannot be helped along it at all. We returned toward evening and made camp. Tried fishing, but got only one strike. Some of us think we are at the canyon, but Spencer thinks not.

Thursday, November 9th. – We awoke to find it drizzling and cold this morning. Got ready as soon as possible and started to cross the river.

A COLD MORNING – WILL'S BLANKET SHIRT.

CHAPTER XII. THE JOURNEY DOWN THE KOOSKOOSKEE

About two hundred yards below the camp there is a fall in the river; and to be sure that we would not be caught in the current (from which escape would be impossible, and which would carry us over the falls), we pulled our rafts up-stream to the head of the eddies and started across from there. Spencer and Keeley took the lead, and made the gravel bar just at the head of the rapid. The left-hand channel was all right, and after running aground on some small rocks, they made the opposite shore and landed. We in turn made the bar, but owing to bad poling our raft turned sidewise in the channel. I jumped out into shallow water, and with a rope tried to hold the stern up-stream, but was promptly swept off my feet, and was wet to the neck before I could regain them. We landed some yards below the other raft. Here we all got off, except Colgate, who could not walk along the rocky shore, and Keeley who was to guide the raft with a pole around the rocks. The rest of us let it down the shore with a long rope. Things went smoothly enough until we got to the large rock in the centre of the stream. The water was so terrific that we thought it best to take Colgate off the raft while passing this place. We helped Colgate up to a small flat just back of the river, and John stayed to assist him. Then two of us took the end of the rope down the river, and one stood just above the rock to snub the raft when it entered the narrow channel. The raft was allowed to run down stream through the worst water, about thirty yards. We then tried to snub it, but its momentum was too much for us, and we were all dragged along through the water and over the rocks for some yards. The next mile was very hard work. We had little space to work in, and were pulled off our feet and dragged a good many times. When about fifty yards from the small eddy which we had picked out as our camping place, we attempted to run the raft between some large rocks. It moved so fast, however, that we could not stop it, and it ran aground on a large gravel bar or point. It was raining hard, and Colgate was so cold that we thought it best to build a fire for him immediately.

THE RIVER NEAR OUR CAMP OF NOVEMBER 9TH.

Keeley would not let his raft down with the rope, but insisted on running the rapids. We didn't think it the best plan, but as it was his raft we said no more about it. Keeley, Spencer, and Abe went back. The last named was to stand at a point where the current made into the shore and throw them a rope in case they failed to land; then they would lead down from there, and thus escape

CHAPTER XII. THE JOURNEY DOWN THE KOOSKOOSKEE

the worst water. John and I unloaded our raft, got in wood for the night, and tried to get a fire going for Colgate. Everything was soaked, and it took us over an hour to get the fire started. Colgate is so stiff that he cannot move. Just before dark Abe came to camp and told us that Keeley had failed to land, and that their raft had upset on a large rock; that they were in a bad position, and as nearly all our provisions are on their raft, we must try to get it off to-night. We gathered all the ropes we could find and hurried up to where they were. The raft was sidewise on the rocks, and about half of it was held under the water by the current. Spencer had a narrow escape from drowning, being nearly washed away when the raft went under. Although we worked hard, we could not budge the raft; so we put a rope to the bow and another to the stern, and fastened them to trees. I built a fire with a piece of dry cedar, while Abe helped Spencer and Keeley to get ashore on the rope. It was now quite dark and we had a rough time walking back to camp. After supper a large fire was built. Spencer has a great knack of making a good fire out of almost anything. We put up our tent and dried our few blankets as best we could. Half our bedding is on the other raft. We had a very hard day, and everyone is completely tired out. It does not rain now and is growing very cold.

Friday, November 10th. – Although fairly tired out last night, we found it difficult to sleep because of the cold. There being insufficient covering and our clothes thoroughly drenched, it is not surprising that we were up and through a hasty breakfast soon after daylight. Upon looking at our raft, just above camp, we found quite a lot of ice on it. It is cold and clear. Immediately after breakfast we

IN THE HEART OF THE BITTER-ROOT MOUNTAINS:
The Story of "the Carlin Hunting Party"

went up to the other raft and found it as firmly lodged as it was the night before. The water seems to have fallen slightly. We hastily constructed a small raft of three logs, held together by ropes. Keeley went on this to the raft in the river. The raft was pulled back, and Spencer went over in the same manner. The canvas covering of the load was loosened, and the provisions were loaded on the small raft and safely landed; the rest of the cargo in like manner. The load being off, we found it possible to dislodge the raft from the rocks, and we pulled it into shore a few yards below. Keeley and Spencer were stiff with cold, so we built a fire and warmed up before proceeding farther.

We decided that it was safer to carry the provisions overland on our backs than to trust them to the raft. Some of us did this while the others let the raft down by ropes, arriving at camp at half past three, tired and hungry. After dinner, having a little daylight left, some got in the night's firewood, while the others made a hasty examination of the river below us for a quarter of a mile. Upon their return they reported the water tremendously swift and that the rocks were more numerous and dangerous than any we had yet seen; in fact, they saw one place ahead that looked impassable, but did not have time to get down near it. This is very disagreeable news, for our ropes are becoming frayed and weak from constant contact with sharp rocks, and will not endure much more work of this kind. In case they should break when we are letting a raft through a bad place, it would mean the probable death of those on board, and the certain loss of the provisions. We are also worried about Colgate, who seems to be failing very rapidly in strength and in mind. He hardly says a word all

CHAPTER XII. THE JOURNEY DOWN THE KOOSKOOSKEE

day except when he is spoken to, or at meal-time, when he is given his food. He sits and gazes for hours with a vacant stare at the river or the rocks. His legs look very bad indeed, and are evidently mortified from the knees down. We found to-day that our flour was getting very low; only about forty pounds are left. We decided to eat no more of it at present, but to live on cornmeal and beans as long as they last. We are out of fresh meat. I tried to catch some fish, but they would not rise. We hope this may be the much-talked-of canyon and that we will soon be through it.

WHERE ONE OF THE RAFTS WAS ABANDONED.

Saturday, November 11th. – It is still cold and clear. We went down the river a long way this morning, and were horrified to find that we were absolutely "stuck." Half a mile below camp is a ledge of rocks, and a rapid through which we cannot take a raft. Below this are two more places still worse. Every one gave his opinion of his own accord, that we could not get our rafts farther down the river. Our position is as follows: We have barely one week's short allowance of flour left. All our other provisions, except a few pounds of cornmeal and beans, and a handful of salt each, are exhausted. The shores of the river are a mass of irregular rocks. Numerous ledges or cliffs, some of them hundreds of feet high, rise vertically above the river and project into it. The hill-sides adjacent are steep and rocky, and covered with dense brush. Many of the ledges are so precipitous that it is all an able-bodied man can do to hang to bushes and climb around them on narrow clefts or steps in the rock. Most of us are considerably weakened from exposure, and are not in a fit condition to walk. Owing to the character of the country and our enfeebled condition, we cannot hope to accomplish more than four or five miles a day on foot. As nearly as we can estimate, we are fifty or fifty-five miles from civilization (Wilson's ranch, twenty miles below the forks). We know nothing whatever of the river ahead of us, of the obstructions we will meet with, or even if we can get through at all by this route. The dreaded Black Canyon is yet before us. Worst of all is the fact that Colgate cannot possibly walk, and it is absolutely impossible to help or carry him around the bad places along the river. His condition grows worse hourly. His legs are in a frightful condition, and the odor that comes from them is almost unendurable. He is perceptibly weaker than he was yesterday, and his mind is so far gone that he has lately appreciated no efforts that have been made to make him comfortable. On our return to camp, at half-past two P.M., we drew to one side and discussed every plan that could be thought of – not a stone was left unturned.

CHAPTER XII. THE JOURNEY DOWN THE KOOSKOOSKEE

If we stay with him, we can do nothing but ease his last moments and bury him, because it is impossible for him ever to get well again. His sickness is, besides, of such a character that he may linger in a stupor or semi-conscious condition for several days, during which a large portion of our remaining provisions will be consumed. We cannot even take him back and leave him with Jerry Johnson, while some of us go out on snowshoes for assistance. With no sign of game in the neighborhood, and the river full of floating ice so that the fish will not rise, were we to leave half our provisions here and one man to care for Colgate, he would probably starve before succor could reach him, while such a drain on the meagre supplies would render the chances considerably less of the others ever reaching civilization. We all feel that it is clearly a case of trying to save five lives, or sacrificing them in order to perform the last sad rites for poor Colgate. To remain longer with Colgate is to jeopardize to the very doors of folly all our lives – not in the cause of humanity, for Colgate is beyond any appreciation of such kindness – but for sentiment solely. We have exhausted every resource, and feel that we have gone to the extreme limit of duty toward Colgate in our endeavors to get him back to civilization. Our own families and friends have now a just claim upon us, and we must save ourselves if possible. We therefore have decided to strike down the river, and, with good luck, some of us may get through, unless we encounter a bad snow-storm. Everyone feels very much dispirited at having to leave Colgate. There was hardly a word spoken by any one to-night.

Sunday, November 12th. – This morning we made up our packs, taking nothing but provisions, two flat stew-

IN THE HEART OF THE BITTER-ROOT MOUNTAINS:
The Story of "the Carlin Hunting Party"

pans that fitted inside one another, the smaller being filled with coffee, and two small frying-pans. Abe will take his camera, which is very light. I cut a roll of exposures out of mine and threw the box away. When we came to cross the river, we found it was not so easy as it looked. We had to reach a small point of rocks, fifty yards below us, on the opposite side of the river. If we failed in this (and the current was against us, as it made in to our side of the river), we would be carried down into the big ledge, and that would be the end of us. Some were in favor of trusting to luck in trying to cross. If we got across, all right; if we didn't, all right too! Others proposed going down on our side of the river, but this was objected to on the ground that this side is likely not to be so open as the south hillside, and would have more snow; besides we would have to cross at the forks anyway, and while we had our rafts we had better cross here. Abe suggested that we fell a very large white pine tree, which stands on the bank and seems to lean toward the river, and by fastening a long rope to the end we could drift half-way across and then pull ashore with our sweeps, while the rope held us from going down the stream. The tree is about forty-four inches in diameter. Keeley began the cutting. Others worked at various things, and I went hunting, in the hope of getting some fresh meat. I saw no fresh signs of game at all except one grouse. On my return I tried fishing, with no better success. Our food for two days had been corn-meal and beans. It snowed a little to-day, and is cloudy and cold. We start on our tramp tomorrow, taking nothing but provisions, guns, and the clothes on our backs. Colgate is very badly off to-night. He has great difficulty in breathing. It would not surprise me

CHAPTER XII. THE JOURNEY DOWN THE KOOSKOOSKEE

at all to see him collapse at any moment. I told him to-day that we could raft no farther and would have to walk, but it seemed to make no impression whatever upon him.

Monday, November 13th. – Daylight found us up and through breakfast, and we were delighted to find it perfectly clear and cool. It took us until one o'clock to fell the big tree, as we had to fall another large tree against it and hitch ropes to its branches, so that it would fall into the river. When it did fall it fairly shook the earth, and, to our disappointment, the top sank fifteen feet under the water. Still, the branches that were available reached nearly-half-way across the river. Abe and Keeley tied one end of the long rope firmly to the limbs as far as they could reach, and the other end was fastened to the raft. We determined to test the strength of the rope and to land Abe on the opposite bank if possible, so that when we crossed with the big load we could throw him a rope, and he could help us land. Abe, Keeley, and I pushed off and got half-way across without the slightest trouble, but had to pull for dear life to get across the current. Landing Abe, we returned for the rest and made the trip safely, although we had a close call to an upset on account of the swift current, which nearly sucked one side of the raft down. After landing, we cut the raft loose, to see where the current would take it; it was whirled downstream for two hundred yards and jammed into a mass of big rocks to the left of the middle of the river.

Poor Colgate was so far gone that he could not remember his family, nor did he make any remarks or request concerning them. We made him as comfortable as we could, left him what necessaries we thought he might require in the brief period he had yet to live, and, shouldering our packs, we started sadly down the river. Although Colgate's head was turned toward us, he made no motion or outcry as he saw us disappear, one by one, around the bend.

We walked over some very rough country until we came to a small creek about two miles down, which we crossed on a log. Our path then led through a rather open flat, and we made camp on a small sand-bar at about four o'clock, having walked two and one-half miles. A small, slanting shelter of pine boughs was made, under which we lay down to sleep.

Tuesday, November 11th. – We had a fairly comfortable camp last night and got several hours' sleep, which was doing well, considering the cold and lack of all covering. After a breakfast of coffee and a small allowance of bread, we resumed our walk down the river at eight o'clock. We shifted and changed our packs a good deal today, as they begin to grow heavy and cut our shoulders. Besides our packs, Keeley carried an axe, and Abe, John, and I had a gun apiece. The first part of the day our route was through a fine flat. We think it is the flat below Bald Mountain, in which they say there is a warm spring. On a small side-hill we found a trail, which led back into the mountains, and by the side of the trail some fairly fresh signs of Indian choppings and "blazes." Some of us were anxious to stop for a day and get an elk, the fresh signs being numerous, but the majority favored going ahead; so we kept on. After leaving the flat, the country began to grow rougher and the side-hills became steep, slippery, rocky, and brushy – all at once, as it were. On one of these side-hills we found an old line chopped out by a surveying party. The walking was very difficult, and we had to use both our hands and feet in climbing. We have kept an eye on the river, and are satisfied that we were very sensible in abandoning the rafts. We have seen a good many places where we could not possibly have taken a raft through. We passed a fall of some six feet, about half-past one o'clock, which had bad rocks above and below it. The river is beautiful: I have never seen such clear-looking water. We walked until three o'clock, having made, we think, five miles. Abe killed a grouse to-day, and I caught two fish weighing half a pound each. We enjoyed them hugely for supper, making broth from the grouse and frying the fish. Our camp is good, and we are fairly comfortable.

A ROUGH SHELTER – BAKING "FRYING-PAN BREAD."

Wednesday, November 15th. – We made a breakfast of tea and a little bread, and started down the river at 8 o'clock. The character of the country was somewhat the same as yesterday – small flats and very difficult sidehills. About noon we passed a fine large creek, which runs through a deep gorge and flows into the river from the south. The lack of nourishing food, loss of sleep, and exposure is beginning to tell on us all; we are very weak and unsteady on our feet. Everything that will lighten our load has been thrown away. During the day we killed three grouse. Abe and John both had watches, but John's stopped after getting it wet in the river a week ago. For safety, Abe had been carrying his watch in his hip-pocket. To-day he slipped and fell down on a rock, smashing the watch. The crystal was pulverized so that it resembled salt. Our last and only timepiece is thus ruined.

We were caught at dark in a miserable flat some distance from the river, making it difficult to obtain water. It began to rain at dark, and continued to rain, sleet, and snow all night. We had trouble to secure firewood, and there is not a tree in the vicinity big enough to shelter any one from the rain, so we got soaking wet and cold, and had no sleep all night. The three grouse were stewed for supper and the bones given to the dogs, which had eaten hardly a mouthful since November 13th. They are about as weak as we are. Daisy, the black dog, seems to be in the poorest condition. I feel that our chances are rather slim of getting out of the mountains. Everyone is tired out and miserable.

Thursday, November 16th. – We got up at daylight and partook of our usual slim breakfast of bread and coffee. The country was very rough today. The first part of our route was over broken, rocky shores. We found more perpendicular bluffs than usual, which we had to climb around. In our weak condition, we found it very hard work to climb up the steep hill-sides. Our guns are a regular nuisance, for we need both hands in climbing. At half past ten we sighted the worst looking bluff we had yet seen, and, upon coming to it, found our way blocked by a large and very rapid creek.

NEAR BLACK CANYON

We stopped here and made a little coffee for lunch. Being unable to find any tree on which to cross the creek, we were obliged to cut one down. Owing to the rain and sleet blowing down the river, the upper side of our tree was icy and slippery. Had any one fallen off, he would have been swept down into the river and drowned. The water is so rapid that it is milky white, from rushing over and between the rocks. Once across, we had a hazardous

IN THE HEART OF THE BITTER-ROOT MOUNTAINS:
The Story of "the Carlin Hunting Party"

climb of an almost perpendicular side-hill for about one thousand feet. It was very slippery and icy, and we were all tired out on reaching the top. It is very lucky that no one fell. Following the ridge for a quarter of a mile, we made a descent to the river again, when, on turning a small point, we came upon the Black Canyon. There was no mistaking it this time! I do not think any view in the mountains ever impressed me as this one did. Not even the magnificent view from the top of the Twisp River divide at the head of Lake Chelan, where the whole Cascade Range of mountains, with its wonderfully varied scenery, can be seen in every direction from seventy-five to one hundred and twenty-five miles. The view did not impress me so much with its grandeur as with an indefinable dread weirdness. It immediately associated itself in my mind with death. The surroundings seemed, for some reason, indescribably well suited to the thought – probably owing to the weakened state of my body and mind. The river before us for several hundred yards was a broad, deep, still pool, which reflected perfectly the steep rocky bank opposite and the muggy sky above. The river gradually narrowed down as it approached the succession of mighty rock-walls, which were so close together that they seemed to meet at the top. A hazy curtain seemed to hang before the tremendous gap, and behind this all seemed black. We could hear the sullen booming of the rapids in the distance, which had a peculiarly unpleasant sound, probably owing to their being enclosed in the huge rocky walls. I should judge that the highest point that we can see from here is at least three thousand feet above the river. I think we all realize now that we have a difficult task ahead. We are very weak, and if Spencer is right in his belief that the canyon is eight

CHAPTER XII. THE JOURNEY DOWN THE KOOSKOOSKEE

or ten miles long, it will take at least two and a half or three days of hard climbing to get through it, if indeed it is passable at all. We were so tired that it was decided that Abe, Spencer, and John should go down the river a short distance and select a suitable camp, while Keeley and I tried the fishing. Never had I seen a finer hole for trout; and in the clear water we could see fish of all sizes lying quietly here and there or swimming lazily about. We had no spoons and no large hooks. We had tied several small flies together, and put a lead weight two feet in front of them to enable us to cast out; then we drew them slowly toward us. We hooked plenty of fish, but they were so large that they broke our hooks time after time. I am certain that one I had almost on shore, when he broke my hook, weighed at least five pounds – it was a Dolly Varden, or bull trout – while Keeley lost one that was considerably larger. After fishing for two hours and losing thirty or more fish and about twenty hooks, we gave up in despair, and returned to camp with one half-pound trout, which Keeley had landed. The others looked so disappointed when we returned to camp with only one small fish that we went out again and managed to catch two more, of nearly one pound apiece. These, added to the grouse Abe had shot, made us a first-rate supper. We stewed the fish, drinking the broth, which was excellent, and divided the flesh evenly in our drinking-cups. If we only had one good, strong trolling spoon, we could catch fifty pounds of fish easily. Our camp is dismally cold and wet, but luckily we have plenty of wood near at hand. We made a big fire for the night. We saw that our best chance for food was fish, and after supper we hunted for something from which to make a spoon. Spencer produced a piece of copper wire, which he used to clean his pipe. Keeley made one spoon from the bowl of a teaspoon, while I made another by hammering out a silver half-dollar. Money is some good in the mountains after all. When finished, they looked very well, and will undoubtedly attract the fish; but we still have to rely on the small hooks to hold them. Upon counting the hooks, I find that we have twenty-four left.

Friday, November 17th. – We started at eight o'clock this morning, determined to do our best toward getting through the canyon. Our route led along a very steep, brushy hill-side. We found an old game trail, which led slanting up the sidehill. We followed this until we were at an elevation of perhaps fifteen hundred feet above the river, when the trail was lost. I guess the game does not pass through the canyon, but strikes back from the river into the hills. We had to be very careful of our footing, as the hillside is so steep that we would probably land in the river, or at any rate over some of the numerous precipices, if we were to slip. The south side of the canyon is vertical at this point, and we believe that this side is so also at the river; it was almost vertical where we passed along to-day. We feel that we were very lucky to have crossed on the raft, for the walls opposite us are impassable. We found more snow to-day than we had yet seen, probably owing to the short time the sun shines in the canyon. "We continued walking with great care all day, and made a difficult descent to the river in order to camp on a small point, where we could get wood and water. Although we worked very hard, we have not accomplished more than two and one-half or three miles. Abe shot a blue grouse to-day. We made camp on the point, and built a shelter to keep out the cold wind that sweeps down the canyon. It is necessary

CHAPTER XII. THE JOURNEY DOWN THE KOOSKOOSKEE

that we should sleep all we possibly can, to keep up our strength. The black dog looked so miserable to-night that I thought it the kindest act all around to kill her. This I did by shooting her in the head with Spencer's revolver. We then hung her up and skinned her, and when the flesh got cold we cut off the best portions and made a strong broth – strong in every sense of the word. Into the broth we put a tablespoonful of flour. The soup was good, but the flesh was tough and strong. Although nearly starved, only one of the three remaining dogs would touch the meat. By our camp is a very large, hollow cedar tree, the base spreading out over six feet. We made a fire in the hollow base. There was a strong draught, so we soon had a regular furnace going. The flames shot out of the top for some distance, and the heat finally became so great that we were obliged to leave our shelter and stretch out on the rocks. We found a portion of last summer's *Spokane Review* and a cleaning-rod for a 45-calibre rifle on the spot where we made our shelter. Evidently someone was up the river this far last summer. We feel somewhat encouraged by these signs of man. Abe took several photographs to-day of the canyon walls and the "crowd." We tried fishing, but had no strikes.

Saturday, November 18th. – We started out by climbing up the side of the canyon, taking every available chance to get forward. The walking is harder than any we have yet had. Many times we were stopped by high perpendicular faces of rock. We had to go up or down for considerable distances to get around some of these; others we had to cross, and trust to luck not to fall. Keeley is particularly good at finding all available footholds and paths. He has been a splendid fellow all through, doing all he could, and not grumbling at all. Expecting to cut around some bad places, we climbed straight up for a long distance, but found nothing better. We got into moose-brush covered with snow, and our feet slipped from under us at every few steps. Nothing seems to do us so much harm in our weak condition as the jarring resulting from a fall. After we got out of the moosebrush we ran into a thicket, and then climbed a snowy side-hill through brush and down timber. Looking back from the top of this ridge, we saw Bald Mountain about fifteen miles to the northeast. At three o'clock we struck what looked like a trail, but it led us to a point where there was a perpendicular descent of several hundred feet; it was evidently not a trail at all. The view from here is extended and grand, but we are not in a condition to admire scenery. We were utterly tired out, and proposed camping. Spencer tried to get to the river, but came back and reported that he could not get down; so we decided to camp about fifty yards farther down, in a bunch of rocks and near a little creek. It took me nearly one hour to work my way down to the creek and bring back a pail of water, but we found a much easier path later. We had difficulty in finding firewood for the night. A few boughs were cut to lie upon, but I fear no one will be able to sleep. We can easily see the rocky bluff just above last night's camp. We have made less than one and one-half miles down the river to-day. Everyone is growing weaker, and the flour is getting very low. Abe killed one grouse to-day, and to-night someone sang, "We'll be angels by and by," and no one seemed to disagree with the singer.

Sunday, November 19th. – John decided to abandon his gun, so he left it hanging to a tree in camp. We felt

CHAPTER XII. THE JOURNEY DOWN THE KOOSKOOSKEE

that we must work hard to-day, which we did. The walking improved, and we found occasional old game trails. We lost much valuable time, however, by following one which took us up into the hills. We passed many bad places, and it is a wonder to me that no one slips and falls, all being so weak. Two of us have no hobnails left in our boots, and three of us are very footsore. We feel encouraged by having seen that we are a good way below Bald Mountain, and we ought not to be more than fifteen miles from the forks of the river, where there is a trail leading down to Wilson's ranch. Fresh deer signs were seen to day. At four o'clock we reached the end of the canyon, and camped near a small sand-bar. We built two large parallel fires, but did not succeed in keeping warm. We have only enough flour left for one more meal [?]. Not being able to sleep, from weakness and cold, I sat thinking of what our friends were doing in the outside world, when my attention was attracted by the two little dogs, Montana and Idaho. Poor little Montana is very far gone, and so weak and thin that it is a surprise to me that she can keep up with us. All the hair is worn from her legs by the sharp rocks. To-night she lay down as close as she could to the fire and extended her four legs, to keep them warm; still she shivered, I suppose from weakness. Idaho, her mate, is much stronger, and seemed to realize Montana s condition, for she came and lay partly on top of her and partly on the outside of her, so as to protect the side exposed to the cold. I do not recall ever having heard of a similar case of animal sympathy.

Monday, November 20th. – For breakfast we ate the last of the bread. We worked for all that was in us to-day, and were favored with pretty good walking in comparison to what we have been having. We were able to keep

IN THE HEART OF THE BITTER-ROOT MOUNTAINS:
The Story of "the Carlin Hunting Party"

near the river a good part of the time, instead of having to continually climb around vertical walls. We staggered a good deal to-day from weakness, and Abe, who has stood it splendidly so far, is also beginning to break down, principally from lack of sleep, having averaged only about one hour a night for seven nights. We found a few frozen hawberries along our route, which we ate. Our violent cravings of hunger have left us somewhat, and our stomachs seem to have accustomed themselves to do with very little. Fully six miles were covered to-day, and camp was made during a cold rain in a damp flat. Abe went to look for deer for half an hour, but saw none, although fresh signs were plentiful in the snow. Keeley caught a fish weighing one pound, of which we made broth, and had that and coffee for supper. It was very difficult to get enough wood to last all night.

Tuesday, November 21st. – We had a little piece of bacon, weighing about one-eighth of a pound, which we used to grease the pan with in baking bread. The flour being exhausted, we made a broth of that this morning. Abe went for deer, but got none, as it began to snow. Most of us are too weak to walk without breakfast, and can barely stagger around. Keeley caught three fish which we ate, and started down the river at eleven o'clock, walking very slowly and often stumbling and falling down. After going about a mile we found a nice fishing-hole. Keeley caught four and I two, making six fine fish in all – a veritable feast. I had no control over my arms. When I whirled the spoon around to throw it into the river, it was just as likely to fly back of or above me. We soon made camp and stewed the fish. The dogs got quite a meal of fish bones, and seemed to feel relieved.

Wednesday, November 22d. – It snowed about two inches during the night, and this morning it was dark

CHAPTER XII. THE JOURNEY DOWN THE KOOSKOOSKEE

and squally. We tried hard to catch fish, but did not get a strike. One small fish kept following Keeley's spoon to the shore, but would not strike. Getting desperate, he shot at it with his revolver, but missed it. Seeing it was no use to fish, we made some tea and started slowly down the river. The majority decided that we would walk no farther after to-day, but would try to build a rude raft if we could find light driftwood that required no cutting from which to build it. Our feet felt as heavy as lead, and falls were frequent. We notice that the hills are getting very low now. Abe, who has been keeping account of our daily progress, estimated that we were about nine or ten miles from the forks this morning. The rapids are no longer dangerous, and most of us feel that, if we had a raft, we could make Wilson's ranch in a day or two at the most. If we could kill no grouse or trout, we could eat one of the dogs to keep up our strength. The walking was rather hard, as we had to leave the river bank to climb around vertical walls of rock several times. We had made, perhaps, one mile when we struck a particularly bad place. I got too high up to cross easily and thus dropped behind the others some distance, but found Abe waiting for me when I got down. I was tempted to throw away my gun, but disliked very much to part with it, as it is my favorite. We continued slowly down along the side-hill, and seeing some hawberries on the river bank, went down to eat them. I said: "Abe, it seems to me that our friends must know of our position, and that they would try to get up this river as far as they could toward us. They certainly know that this is the route we are most likely to take, and that we must be working down this way!" Abe said in reply, "I have thought it all over and believe they will send someone; but

IN THE HEART OF THE BITTER-ROOT MOUNTAINS:
The Story of "the Carlin Hunting Party"

I allow them three or four days yet." On turning the next point, we saw two men hurrying toward us. Thinking they were of our party I said, "I wonder what's the matter? Perhaps they have seen a deer and want us to shoot it!" but he replied, "I am afraid someone has fallen into the river." As they approached nearer, we saw they were not of our party, and a moment later Abe recognized our old-time shooting chum, Sergt. Guy Norton, of the Fourth Cavalry. With him was Lieut. Charles P. Elliott. It expresses it mildly to say we were overjoyed to see them. Our tired limbs seemed filled with new life, and we followed them briskly to their first boat, about two hundred yards below. Abe, who was very much interested in his estimate of distances, asked Mr. Elliott how far it was to the "forks," and learned, with much satisfaction, that the confluence of the south fork with the Kooskooskee was about seven miles distant. When we arrived where Mr. Elliott's boat was lying, we found the rest of our party and two soldiers – Sergt. Smart and Private Norlin, of Mr. Elliott's company – and three civilian boatmen, Messrs. Lamonthe, Burke, and Winn. They had a fire started and oatmeal and bacon cooking when we arrived. Mr. Elliott advised us to eat moderately at first, until we gradually accustomed ourselves again to food. While enjoying our first meal, we learned all the details of the meeting of the two parties. Mr. Elliott's party was making its way up the river with two boat-loads of provisions. So swift and rough was the water that a portage was necessary at nearly every rapid. They had gotten the smaller boat over the last rapid below; and while the balance of the party returned for the other boat, Mr. Elliott and Roary Burke sat down on a rock near the first boat and waited for them. While thus

CHAPTER XII. THE JOURNEY DOWN THE KOOSKOOSKEE

seated, their attention was attracted by the barking of Winn's dog, and when they looked around Burke saw one of our little white terriers through an opening under the rocks. Not knowing what it was, Mr. Elliott asked for a gun, but soon discovered that what he saw was a small white dog. The terrier "Idaho" soon made her presence known by violent barking. At the same time Spencer, who had, however, seen the two men first, appeared above the rocks, followed closely by John and Keeley.

Mr. Elliott, seeing Spencer, accosted him with: "Hello! Who in God's name are you?"

Spencer replied: "My name is Spencer, the guide of the Carlin party. Who are you?

After informing Spencer that a rescuing party was at hand, Mr. Elliott asked, "How is everybody?" to which Spencer replied, "All well, but hungry as h – l!"

The rest of Mr. Elliott's party having come up in the meantime, he left instructions to prepare a meal for the rescued party, and came forward with Sergt. Norton, as already related.

Mr. Elliott immediately decided to send a courier with dispatches to Captain Boutelle at Weippe, and selected Mr. Winn. We were kindly given permission to send telegrams to our relatives and friends with the courier. We find that new ranches have been built on the river above Wilson's, and that we are only five miles from the nearest cabin (King's). Mr. Winn will walk down the river to Hinds and Burke's ranch, and thence ride by trail to Weippe.

CHAPTER XIII.

THE RESCUE AND DISBANDMENT

AFTER we had taken some refreshments on the river bank, all the provisions were ordered to be loaded in the boat, and the whole party, rescuers and rescued, returned to Mr. Elliott's last camp, half a mile below.

Canvas stretched over poles afforded shelter, and while the civilians of Mr. Elliott's party went down the river to look for raft timber, the soldiers made camp comfortable and set about preparing the evening meal. No one who has never gone through a similar experience can imagine the feeling of rest, relief, and security that we felt sitting by the warm camp fire, with kind friends about us and plenty of food in sight.

Mr. Elliott inquired minutely about Colgate, and was anxious to go after him and bring him out dead or alive. It was with great difficulty that we were able to persuade him that such a course was not only extremely dangerous but probably impossible. From our knowledge of the river and the region we had just passed through, we knew the

CHAPTER XIII. THE RESCUE AND DISBANDMENT

river was not navigable for boats above the mouth of the canyon, and ice-floes were already forming, so that boating would probably have been impracticable above the point Mr. Elliott had reached when we met him. Assuming that to be the case, it would have been necessary to have the men who would volunteer to go, carry twenty days' provisions on their backs and pass over the same route we had just travelled. Had no snow fallen during that time, they would in all probability have been able to pass through the canyon and reach the point where Colgate was last seen, but it would probably have been eighteen or twenty days after we had left him, and according to Dr. Webb's statement, which appears elsewhere, Colgate would then have been dead over fifteen days.* It would have been impossible in any case to bring out Colgate's body, as the canyon is absolutely impassable to the strongest men if burdened by such a load as Colgate's body would have been. Had snow fallen at any time while the men were in or above the canyon, they would have been hopelessly imprisoned and certainly lost, as there is no game of any kind in the canyon, and the snow, on the almost precipitous walls, would have rendered travelling so dangerous as to be practically impossible.

In view of the dangerous nature of such a trip, and the fact that the burial of the body, if found, would be all the expedition could accomplish, Mr. Elliott wisely decided with us that the results did not warrant the jeopardizing of the lives of the valuable men who readily volunteered to go. As it happened, four inches of snow fell at our camp the following day, and we believe that double that amount

---
* See page 173

IN THE HEART OF THE BITTER-ROOT MOUNTAINS:
The Story of "the Carlin Hunting Party"

must have fallen in the canyon, which is much higher above sea level. It is therefore almost certain that an attempt to reach Colgate at that time would not only have resulted in failure, but might have ended disastrously.

In order that the boats could be made available to carry passengers, it was necessary to build a large raft to transport the provisions. The construction of the raft took nearly three days. This afforded us an admirable opportunity for recuperating and resting.

Mr. Elliott was exceptionally kind and considerate, and repeatedly sacrificed his own comfort for us by giving us his blankets at night while he endeavored to sleep by the camp fire. The first night in camp was, and no doubt always will be, a memorable night to us. For the first time in ten days we had a comfortable bed under shelter, and the sleep – the refreshing sleep which we so badly needed – was most delightful.

The weather was very disagreeable. It snowed and sleeted constantly, but we were all comfortable under the protecting canvas, and happy in the thought that the anxiety of our friends would soon be changed into joy at the news that we were safe.

The day after we met Mr. Elliott, two trappers who were making a trip up the river reached the point where the men were building the raft. They had a canoe with a winter's supply of provisions, but became discouraged on account of the numerous falls and swift current of the river, and decided to return to the "forks" and go up the south fork of the Kooskooskee.

The raft being finished on Saturday, November 25th, the provisions were moved down and loaded on it. Mr. El-

CHAPTER XIII. THE RESCUE AND DISBANDMENT

liott, John, Spencer, and Lamonthe took the larger of the two boats, and Norton, Keeley, Will, and Abe the smaller one. The rest of the party manned the raft.

The start was made about eleven o'clock. The journey down the river in the boats was very interesting, and had the weather been fair and not quite so cold it would have been greatly enjoyed.

The current, while not quite so swift as higher up the river, carried the boats along at a marvellous speed, and, where the water was shallow, we could see the boulders shoot by beneath us, producing an effect similar to that of travelling on a railway train.

The river widened rapidly, the mountains on each side gradually became lower, and the fall of the river less. Shortly after we started, we passed the sluices and ruins of an old placer mining camp, and soon afterward passed the first cabin, belonging to a man named King. Here Mr. Elliott stopped, and returned some tools that had been previously borrowed. Continuing down the river a couple of miles, we reached "the forks." Here the South Fork flows into the Kooskooskee. Several small falls were safely passed, but at about three o'clock, after having made a total run of perhaps twelve miles, we struck an ice floe which obstructed the river for several hundred yards. Mr. Elliott made an examination and found that the ice had formed an arch at the lower end of the floe, which if broken through, might allow the ice to pass off.

While his party were engaged in the work of disrupting the ice gorge, our party travelled down the river on foot, two and a half miles, to a ranch belonging to Roary Burke and F. M. Hinds. Mr. Hinds was at home and welcomed us very kindly. In half an hour we sat down to an excellent meal, to which we did ample justice. At sundown Mr. Elliott and party arrived with the raft and boats, having successfully broken through the ice-floe. The ice passing out, after the breaking of the arch, was a spectacle well worth seeing – huge masses rising above the surface of the water, and rolling over and over as the water became shallower below the pool where the gorge had formed.

Messrs. Hinds and Burke, in the role of hosts, acquitted themselves admirably, and the evening was pleasantly spent; cards, stories, and the incidents of the trip furnishing ample means of diversion.

It rained the following day, and as we were very comfortable in the capacious, well-built cabin, it was decided to remain there until the next day. In the morning, Messrs. Elliott, Burke, and Freeman and Sergeant Norton went hunting, leaving at daylight, while the rest of us remained indoors and passed a quiet, restful day. At noon the hunters returned, having been unsuccessful in securing venison, but bringing in several grouse.

The next day, November 27th, at eight o'clock in the morning, we resumed our journey down the river. It rained all day, but we made excellent progress notwithstanding. After floating about eight miles down the river, we arrived at Kooskia, a post-office where mails are received once a week. The postmaster had apples for sale, and we availed ourselves of the opportunity to purchase some, and enjoyed them immensely.

The river constantly widened, and we passed into an open, rolling country almost destitute of timber. Only two stops were necessary to pass by dangerous rapids. At two

CHAPTER XIII. THE RESCUE AND DISBANDMENT

o'clock we reached Kamai, a Nez Perces Indian village, having made a run of about twenty miles.

Here we found an Indian trader's store, where we purchased some butter, cheese, and milk, which on trips of this character are always regarded as luxuries. We re-embarked and continued down the river about a mile, where we found a favorable place and made camp.

It continued to rain, but a comfortable camp, with two large fires, had a cheering effect, and everybody was happy. Although it was still raining in the morning, we broke camp at daybreak and continued down the river. Several dangerous rapids were passed, in one of which the raft came very near overturning. At another, the large boat, then occupied by Mr. Elliott, Will, John, and Lamonthe, was carried broadside against a large boulder and almost swamped. It was, however, pushed off in the nick of time, and it passed through the rapids with nearly a foot of water surging about in its bottom.

About one o'clock of that day, we reached Greer's Ferry. Here Mr. Elliott met and reported to Captain Boutelle. We also met at this point Dr. Carter and Lieutenant Voorhees. The latter was an old acquaintance of Will's, and their meeting was to Will entirely unexpected. Mr. Voorhees was stationed at Fort Walla Walla, Wash , and had volunteered his services. In command of twenty picked men and with several wagon-loads of supplies, he had arrived at Greer's Ferry several days before, only to learn that the "lost party" had been located by Mr. Elliott, and was coming down the river.

An hour was spent at Greer's Ferry, when we re-embarked, and continued down the river. At four o'clock, after

IN THE HEART OF THE BITTER-ROOT MOUNTAINS:
The Story of "the Carlin Hunting Party"

having made a run of about eighteen miles, we reached the North Fork of the Clearwater. Here we made camp in the rain. Acting under orders from Captain Boutelle, Mr. Elliott and party waited at that point until Captain Boutelle joined him a couple of days later, while our party engaged passage from two ranchers in a covered wagon and travelled the following day to Snell's mill, eight miles distant.

Remaining there with Mr. Gainer overnight, we started the following morning on horseback for Kendrick. Six inches of snow had fallen during the night, and the morning was cold and clear. Mr. Elliott had kindly supplied us with warm army overcoats, so we had no difficulty in keeping comfortable.

It was fourteen miles to Kendrick. The last five miles were through a gulch or canyon leading from an elevated plateau to the valley of Bear Creek, which the railway follows. That portion of the highway is cut into steep hillsides, forming the sides of the gulch. The recent rain had swollen the stream and caused several landslides, making the road almost impassable at places. We, however, moved along without much difficulty, arriving in Kendrick at one o'clock – just in time to enjoy the Thanksgiving Day dinner at the St. Elmo Hotel.

General Carlin had been in Kendrick for several days, awaiting the arrival of the party, and the meeting of father and son was very affecting. A large crowd of interested spectators had gathered, which soon dispersed after our arrival.

The morning's ride in the crisp bracing air, after a week of rainy weather and insufficient exercise, proved very beneficial to all.

CHAPTER XIII. THE RESCUE AND DISBANDMENT

The following morning, December 1st, the whole party, including General Carlin, left for Spokane, where we arrived at about two o'clock. We were met at the depot by a great many friends, whose warm congratulations and hearty shaking of the hand conveyed the sincerity of their feelings.

THE RETURN TO KENDRICK

The following day Dr. Webb, George Colgate's physician, was found. All the details of Colgate's illness and his condition at the time he was last seen were related to him, and upon request he made the following statement in writing:

Mr. Colgate came to me from Post Falls last summer and I placed him in the Sacred Heart Hospital, where he remained about three weeks, and then returned to Idaho. Early last fall he again came to me to be examined and said, if he was well enough, he would start on a hunting-trip as cook. Mr. Colgate was troubled with an enlarged prostate and chronic inflammation of the bladder, and had been for twenty years compelled to use catheters to relieve the bladder. I told him he could make the trip, but to continue the use of the catheters; and from the history of the case and symptoms described by the Carlin party, I am satisfied Colgate's illness would have resulted fatally under any circumstances, and when he was left behind in the condition described, he could not have survived twenty-four hours.

W. Q. WEBB.
SPOKANE, WASH., December 4th, 1893.

Soon after our arrival we were met at the Hotel Spokane by Mrs. Colgate, Charles Colgate her eldest son, and several friends of the family from Post Falls. Will spent over three hours with them, telling the entire narrative of the trip, and all the circumstances concerning Mr. Colgate. At the noon hour General Carlin invited them to lunch, and after lunch a half-hour more was spent in relating additional details. After hearing the whole story, the accompanying friends were satisfied that all was done that could possibly have been done for Mr. Colgate.

It was suggested that a searching party be sent out for the body, but we strenuously advised against such a course, on account of the great danger and hardships incident to such an undertaking at that unfavorable season of the year. Will, however, volunteered his services and

CHAPTER XIII. THE RESCUE AND DISBANDMENT

assistance in the spring, when a party could undertake such a trip with a reasonable hope of success.

Financially, as well as otherwise, the trip proved disastrous. Ben Keeley made considerable trouble by being dissatisfied, and insisting on being paid a much larger sum than was originally agreed upon. Although Will offered to replace his personal property lost on the trip, besides paying the stipulated $250, he was dissatisfied, and finding he could not succeed in getting more, he accepted Will's offer, but went away angry, and subsequently, when the party had disbanded, circulated the most cruel and malicious falsehoods concerning them. Although one of the rescued, he had the audacity to claim the reward offered by General Carlin for the rescue of the party, and threatened to bring a civil action against him for it.

All the camp equipage, except what was left with Jerry Johnson and what the party carried out with them, was irretrievably lost. The horses probably perished from starvation during the winter. A portion of the equipment that had been hired for the trip, and which was returnable to the owners, had to be paid for. To all these pecuniary losses must be added the expense of the relief expeditions sent out by General Carlin, which amounted to several thousand dollars.

On December 6th, after adjusting a few remaining business matters relative to the trip, the party disbanded.

CONCLUSION

With its disbandment, the story of the "Carlin Hunting Party" ends. As a hunting party proper, it met with very indifferent success. On account of the inclement weather, what game was taken was secured at the sacrifice of every personal comfort and much exposure. The disasters which befell the party are distinctly and directly traceable to a combination of two unfortunate circumstances: the premature fall of heavy snows in the mountains, and the complete disability of George Colgate after the party had reached its destination. Had either of these misfortunes befallen the party singly, there probably would have been no more serious consequences than a little inconvenience or exposure for the members of the party; but both occurring simultaneously, the party found every resource by which the one misfortune could be averted, handicapped or rendered impracticable by the other. The premature fall of the winter snows was a circumstance that could not, of course, have been anticipated; but the disability of Colgate was unquestionably due to his own folly in leaving behind the instruments on which his existence depended. By maintaining silence during the long journey into the woods, when a word would have halted the party and enabled them to inaugurate measures for his relief, he not only grievously wronged the rest of the party from an ethical standpoint, but also, as subsequent events proved, wilfully threw away the only chance of saving his life and thereby sealed his own fate. When the party first realized the painful situation in which his conduct had placed them, they were, naturally, much chagrined; and although Colgate was a burden to them after the time they reached their permanent camp on the Kooskooskee, he was treated with the utmost kindness, and, as he grew worse, nursed with the greatest care. When the return was attempted on Oct. 10th, had it not been for Colgate's complete disability the party would in all probability have continued their journey homeward on snowshoes over the Lo-Lo trail, arriving at Kendrick by October 20th. The anxiety of their friends and the expense of the relief expeditions would thus have been avoided, and the obligation of hazarding that month of privation and exposure occasioned by the journey down the Kooskooskee – the danger and hardships of which are as yet but half told – would not have devolved upon them. It is doubtful if any other party of the same character and organized for a similar purpose was ever called upon to face such painful and desperate situations. Every emergency and crisis was, however, squarely and bravely met, and carefully considered and discussed by the whole party in a most serious and rational manner, and the conclusions reached by them were prompted by a judgment based upon a knowledge of all the attending circumstances. That the rest of the party succeeded in effecting their escape down the Kooskooskee without serious or fatal accident falls little short of the miraculous.

APPENDIX A.
THE RELIEF EXPEDITIONS

EARLY in November, 1893, after deep snows had been reported in the mountains, Mr. John L. Randle, of Spokane, Wash., received the following characteristic and significant letter from William H. Wright, of Missoula, Mont.:

> If Spencer has not got out of the mountains before now, he will not get out before spring – not that way [*via* Kendrick], as the snow is from four to six feet deep in the mountains, and it is impossible to get out any horses, unless it is this way [*via* Missoula], and then one could not do so unless they went in from this way and took a pack train of oats. It has snowed for over a month on the range. I cam eout with a party in about two feet of snow. Two men going out about a week ago, started with six horses and got out with two, and would not have got out then only for some Indians, who helped them. Do you know of any one who knows where they [the Carlin party] were going and how much grub they took? How many horses did they take? General Carlin had better send out a relief party to hunt them up. If you see him, tell him I really think so, for if they have not got out they will not, unless they come on snowshoes.

As Mr. Wright is a well-known professional guide and a partner of Martin P. Spencer, the guide of the Carlin party, the letter was deemed highly important and promptly handed to Capt. Louis Merriam, U. S. A., also of Spokane. Captain Merriam immediately telegraphed

APPENDIX A.

Mr. Wright for further particulars, and received a reply to the effect that nothing had been heard of the Carlin party, and that six feet of snow was reported in the mountains. Captain Merriam immediately telegraphed General Carlin, apprising him of the situation. This took place on November 7th. The same evening General Carlin replied as follows:

> "Thanks for information. If possible, go to Missoula and ask Colonel Burt, commandant at Fort Missoula, for a party of men, pack animals, subsistence, and guide, and go to relief of Will and party. I will pay all expenses."

On account of a washout on the Northern Pacific Railroad, Captain Merriam was delayed at Hope, Idaho, until Lieutenant Martin, aide-de-camp of General Carlin, had reached the same point from Vancouver *en route* to Missoula with identical instructions. Captain Merriam thereupon returned to Spokane to direct the movements of the other parties, while Lieutenant Martin pushed his way eastward toward Missoula, where he arrived on the morning of November 10th. After consultation with Major McKibbin (Colonel Burt being at that time absent), it was decided to send a strong relief party into the mountains.

In the mean time Lieut. Charles P. Elliott, of Troop E, Fourth United States Cavalry, hearing of General Carlin's apprehension for the safety of his son and party, kindly volunteered his services to go to their rescue. Accompanied by Sergeant Smart and Privates Markland, Norlin, and Ruhl, they arrived in Spokane from Vancouver Barracks on November 9th. His instructions were to go *via* Fort Sherman, increase his command to ten men,

IN THE HEART OF THE BITTER-ROOT MOUNTAINS:
The Story of "the Carlin Hunting Party"

and complete his supplies for a winter's campaign, and then proceed to Saltese, Mont., *via* Old Mission, and co-operate with the relief party from Missoula. On reaching Old Mission, he found telegraphic orders awaiting him, recalling him to Fort Sherman, and instructing him to proceed to Kendrick, Idaho, join Lieutenant Overton's party at that point, and endeavor to penetrate the Clearwater wilderness from the west.

Lieutenant Overton, of the Fourth Cavalry, with four troopers and a pack-train, had already arrived at Kendrick *via* Colfax and moved on toward Weippe. Lieutenant Elliott, on his arrival at Kendrick, proceeded at once to Weippe, where he found Lieutenant Overton busily engaged in preparing for a journey over the Lo-Lo trail. Lieutenant Elliott, on the other hand, resolved to attempt an ascent of the Kooskooskee, and on the morning of November 14th started for Kamai. The same day Capt. F. A. Boutelle arrived at Weippe and assumed command of all the military parties entering the mountains from the east.

While these movements were taking place on the western border of the Clearwater wilderness, a detachment of fifty-three men, under the command of Captain Andrews, of Company F, Twenty-fifth Infantry, was penetrating the same region from the east. This force left Fort Missoula on the afternoon of the 10th of November, taking three escort-wagons and rations for fifteen days. They were followed by Lieutenant Devol, Lieutenant Martin, William H. Wright (guide), two packers, one supply wagon, and two pack-mules. Great difficulty was experienced in passing the numerous fords of the Lou-Lou fork, and

APPENDIX A.

the supply-wagon was finally abandoned and the stores transferred to the pack-mules. After reaching the Lou-Lou warm springs, on November 12th, a reconnoissance was made to the divide, and on the following day another to the Kooskooskee. Three stations, num-bered 1, 2, and 3, were then established on the trail west of the Warm Springs, the last being on the Kooskooskee. Five men and two pack-mules were to occupy each station and make daily trips over the intermediate portions of the trail, keeping it open and transferring provisions, orders, etc. These stations were established on November 15th, and the following day Mr. Wright, accompanied by Lieutenant Caldwell and two men, with four pack-mules, started down the old Indian trail along the river toward the camp of the Carlin party. The ice in the bed of the river, and the difficult fords, in which the mules were swept off their feet by the swift current, made their progress so slow that at the end of six hours they found they had only accomplished two miles. Owing to the necessity of cutting loose the packs in order to save the mules from drowning when they fell in the river, nearly all their provisions and forage had been lost. Mr. Wright lost his gun, and came very near being drowned by his horse sliping in the river and falling upon him. Under these circumstances the route down the river was pronounced impracticable, and the party returned to Station No. 3, on the river, whence they had started in the morning. The next morning, November 17th, the same party attempted to reach the Carlin party's camp by way of the Lo-Lo trail over the mountains. No serious difficulty was experienced for the first five or six miles, except that the snow became deeper and deeper as they proceeded. At that distance, however, they found the snow on the north hill-sides so soft that the horses could not travel in it, while the south hill-sides were so steep as to be absolutely impracticable for horses. They were consequently compelled to return again to Station No. 3, and decided to send to Captain Andrews for enough men and mules to establish two more camps beyond the Kooskooskee, and then attempt to reach the Carlin camp on snowshoes. Captain Andrews was at Station No. 1, and on the arrival of Lieutenant Martin and Mr. Wright, he informed them that high water had rendered the wagon-road impracticable, and that their supplies were cut off. Only two days' provisions remained, and a snowstorm was approaching. Captain Andrews, therefore, sent out couriers to recall the men at the other stations, and on the night of November 18th the whole force had collected at the Warm Springs. The next morning a snowstorm was raging, and it was decided to return at once to Fort Missoula. The high water still rendered the wagon-road impracticable, and all the wagons and many of the supplies had to be abandoned. Everything that could be taken was carried on the pack animals over the high-water trail, which was extremely dangerous at that season of the year. Five of the mules at different times lost their footing and rolled headlong down the steep sides of the mountains, along which the trail passed. One of these rolled a distance of at least five hundred feet, striking the snow at intervals of about every fifty feet. He was found shortly afterward browsing on the brush near where he had fallen, in the most unconcerned manner, but very little of his pack was recovered. Two of the other mules Avere, however, killed. The expedition returned to Fort Missoula on November 24th, and two days afterward the telegraph announced the rescue of the party.

While Captain Andrews' command was struggling in the deep snow on the east, Lieutenant Overton was pushing his way laboriously into the mountains on the west. Lieutenant Elliott had, in the mean time, proceeded to Pete King Bar, on the Kooskooskee, where several days were spent in building two boats, When these were completed, provisions for an all-winter campaign were loaded into them, and the journey up the river begun. At noon of the second day, November 22d, they had reached a point about five miles above King's cabin and about seven miles above the confluence of the Kooskooskee and its south fork, where they met the half-famished survivors of the Carlin party, as already described.

Upon the receipt of the dispatches sent by Lieutenant Elliott, to the effect that the Carlin party had been found, all the search and relief expeditions were immediately recalled.

APPENDIX B.
THE PHENOMENAL PRECIPITATION OF RAIN AND SNOW IN THE FALL OF 1893

THE vast region between the Coeur d'Alene and Bitter Root Mountains on the east and the Cascade Range on the west, was subjected to a most phenomenal rainfall in the autumn and early winter of the year 1893. It was naturally more conspicuous and more carefully noted in the agricultural sections of the region where, in many instances, the early, heavy, and incessant rains seriously interfered with the harvesting and housing of the crops. The Palouse country – famous the world over for its productiveness – lying directly west of the Bitter-Root Mountains and adjacent to them, was, for the first time in the recollection of the oldest inhabitants, deluged with rain. The ground soon became soft and miry, so that it was impossible to haul the grain out of the fields after it had been harvested. Consequently over two hundred thousand bushels of grain soured and were lost in the fields of this section alone. The deepest snow ever known fell in the mountains. In the Cascades, authenticated depths of thirty to thirty-five feet were reported, and in the Bitter-Root and Coeur d'Alene Mountains corresponding depths of twenty to twenty-five feet. It is well known by the ranchers and mountaineers living on the outskirts of the Clearwater wilder-ness, that the winter snows usually begin to fall after the 15th of October, and that it is unsafe to remain in the mountains later than that time. There are, however, a number of instances in which prospectors and hunters have succeeded in getting out of the mountains as late as the last of October. Among these may be mentioned the case of Dr. C. S. Penfield, of Spokane, Wash., who hunted in the Warm Springs locality on the Kooskooskee the previous year (1892) and in 1891. On the latter occasion he returned over the Lo-Lo trail, reaching Kendrick, after encountering only two feet of snow, as late as October 23d.

In 1893, however, the snows in the Bitter-Root Mountains began to fall as early as September 18th. No apprehension was felt so early in the fall, and it was not until about the 5th of October that the steady rain and snows caused alarm to persons belated in the mountains.

In September, Messrs. Larson and Houghton assisted Jerry Johnson and Ben Keeley to "pack" in the winter's supply of provisions to their cabin, near the Warm Springs on the Kooskooskee. On September 27th, the day after the Carlin party had arrived and made their camp, Messrs. Larson and Houghton started to return to Missoula with a number of the pack animals. It will be remembered that on this day the prolonged rainstorm began, as noted by the Carlin party. After leaving the river bottom, Messrs. Larson and Hough-ton found themselves in a raging snowstorm, which, continuing with unabating fury, rapidly increased the depth of the snow on the trail.

At one time during their journey, notwithstanding that their horses carried little or no burden, they had almost abandoned them, their progress being so slow and difficult. After four days of continuous floundering in the snow, during which time the snow had fallen to a depth of three feet, they reached the Lou-Lou Warm Springs, in Montana, in a state of complete exhaustion.

By the 10th of October the snow was five feet deep on the Lo-Lo trail. When the relief expeditions endeavored to pass the mountains early in November, the snows had piled up to a depth of eight to ten feet.

In the light of these facts, it would appear that the Lo-Lo trail became impassable for horses on account of the deep snow about the time the Carlin party had reached their destination on the Kooskooskee.

APPENDIX C.
THE COLGATE SEARCHING PARTIES

ON December 27th, 1893, a bottle containing a letter purporting to have been written by George Colgate, and bearing date November 27th, was taken from the Snake River near Penewawa, sixty miles below Lewiston, Idaho. Notwithstanding that it was impossible to properly authenticate the letter, and that it contained the phrase, " Lost Carlin Party" (which was of newspaper origin), many persons living in the neighborhood of Post Falls and Kendrick, believed that it was written by Colgate.

Contrary to the advice of every one who was acquainted with the dangerous character of such an undertaking in midwinter, seven distinct parties were organized to search for and bring out Colgate or his remains. With inadequate outfits, and unacquainted with the character of the country, the most successful of these spent two months in the mountains, enduring the most painful hardship and exposure, only to find that the deep snow rendered the success of their undertaking hopeless.

In March, 1894, one of these parties met with a fatal accident. Four men had gone up the river to trap and look for Colgate. They ascended the river in a canoe to a point near the Black Can-yon but finding the snow still very deep and their progress slow and laborious, they decided to return. An attempt was made to run the rapids in the canoe, but they had gone only a short distance when the canoe ran into a log and was smashed. Some of their supplies were lost, but they removed the remainder to the nearest bank and improvised a rude raft. Starting out on this, with two men at each end, they had proceeded only about eighty rods when the raft struck a rock in the river, and the two men at the forward end of the raft were thrown into the rapid current. Although they were strong, active men, and good swimmers, they failed to reach the shore, and were drowned. The other two men clung to the raft and the rocks, and, by cutting one log of the raft loose at a time and tying them together with their coats and shirts, managed, after two hours of peril, to reach the shore. The names of the two men lost are Loyal C. Hallam and Harry Gamble. The former was about twenty-seven years of age, and had a mother and sister living at Humboldt, Neb.; the latter was of about the same age, and came from Baker City, Ore. The bodies of both men were subsequently found, – one near Kooskia P. O., and the other near Lapwai, where they were buried. Both men were unmarried.

In the spring of 1894, Messrs. Carlin and Him-melwright engaged Martin P. Spencer to under-take a journey to the cabin of Jerry Johnson at the earliest date at which the journey could be made with safety. The object of the expedition was to search for the remains of George Colgate, and recover the camp equipage, etc., which had been left with Johnson. Mr. Spencer secured for companions, his partner, William H. Wright, and George R.

Ogden, of Missoula, Mont., and started into the mountains on May 21st. After experiencing considerable difficulty with snow (which at places was twenty feet deep, but packed so that the horses were enabled to walk over it) and high water, they reached Jerry Johnson's cabin on June 7th. " Old Jerry" was delighted to see them, having endured seven long months of solitude. His provisions were almost exhausted. The snow had been ten feet deep on the little flat where his cabin stood, and where the Carlin Party had encamped the preceding fall. For two and a half months he had been imprisoned in his cabin by the soft snow, coming out only to secure necessary firewood, which was near at hand. His little terrier dog, " Tootsey," had been his sole companion all winter. After the snow had melted sufficiently, he secured some game, and succeeded in trapping a few fur-bearing animals.

All the horses which the Carlin Party had left there, and three belonging to Johnson, had died during the winter, but their trophies and camp equipage, which had been left in the cabin in Johnson's care, were found in good condition.

On June 10th, the party started down the river in search of Colgate's remains, taking two pack animals. Two days of difficult work over an old trail, and the loss of one of the pack animals, brought them to a point eighteen miles below Johnson's cabin. Here the river bank became impracticable for horses. Starting out the next morning on foot, six hours of hard climbing were required in order to pass over the remaining five miles to the last camp of the Carlin Party. On their arrival at that point, they saw the tent and several blankets caught in some driftwood in

IN THE HEART OF THE BITTER-ROOT MOUNTAINS:
The Story of "the Carlin Hunting Party"

an eddy. Near the same place were more blankets, on the sand, about five feet from the edge of the water. About a hundred yards farther down, and near the water's edge, Spencer found a roll of blankets weighted down by a boulder, which he at once recognized as the roll which had been done up for Colgate by the party the previous fall. They had never been unrolled, and the rope which had bound them to Colgate's back still held the roll together at one end. The other end of the rope was much frayed, as though worn through by rubbing against the ragged edge of a rock. One of Colgate's shirts was wrapped up inside the roll. About half a mile farther down the river, a sleeve, believed to belong to the corduroy coat which Col-gate wore, was found hanging on the brush in the river. Although the search was prosecuted with the utmost care and diligence for three miles farther down the river, nothing more of the unfortunate Colgate was revealed. Returning to Jerry Johnson's cabin, the party rested two days and then returned to Missoula, where they arrived on June 21st.

The facts developed by this expedition would seem to indicate:

1. That the unfortunate man was unable to move any appreciable distance from the spot where he was last seen.
2. That since his blankets had not been unrolled, he probably never regained the full power of his faculties, but remained in the stupor or semi-conscious condition he was in until his death.
3. That all the facts ascertained by this expedition, as well as his condition and all the circumstanc-

es surrounding him when last seen, indicate almost to a certainty that George Colgate died within twenty-four hours after the departure of the other members of the party; and from the nature of his ailment, death must have come to him without conscious pain.

4. – That the high water in the spring carried the body down stream.

United States Army expeditions were sent out by the Department of the Columbia to explore the St. Joseph and Clearwater River basins. To one of these expeditions, in command of Lieut. James A. Leyden, was assigned the territory north of the Lo-Lo trail, and to the other, in command of Lieut. Charles P. Elliott, the region south of the Lo-Lo trail. During the month of August, while on the Kooskooskee River, Lieut. Elliott found and buried the remains of George Colgate. The unfortunate man's remains were found about four miles farther down the river than the Spencer-Wright searching party had gone, and about eight miles below the place where they had found his blankets the preceding June.

APPENDIX D.
BIOGRAPHICAL

WILLIAM EDWARD CARLIN was born in Buffalo, N. Y., July 26th, 1866. From early childhood he manifested the greatest interest in firearms and all manner of field and water sports. His father, the well-known army officer, recently retired from service – Brig.-Gen. William P. Carlin – was for many years stationed in the Dakotas, and after-ward in the far Northwest, at Fort Sherman, Idaho; and being an ardent lover of sport and an enthusiastic shooter himself, his son, profiting by " precept and example," soon became proficient in the use of the shotgun and rifle.

Early in 1888, Mr. Carlin became interested in pistol and revolver shooting, and now ranks among the leading amateur pistol shots of the country. Mr. Carlin shoots solely for the amusement it affords him; and as he is not seeking notoriety, only a few of his intimate friends have witnessed his shooting and enjoyed – friendly matches with him. In fact, his wife who is also a good shot and an enthusiast on shooting matters – is frequently his sole companion when he practises at the target.

Mr. Carlin loves the woods, and is happy when in the society of congenial spirits in some isolated game country.

During his life in the Northwest since 1871, he has accompanied numberless hunting parties, and was a member of the expedition under Lieut. James A. Leyden, U. S. A., which penetrated into the Lake Chelan and Colville region of northern Washington in 1889, for the purpose of exploring the mountain passes in that district.

In addition to his shooting accomplishments, Mr. Carlin is an expert fisherman, and an amateur photographer of large and varied experience in landscape work. He has the happy faculty of making many and fast friends wherever he is. The few who are fortunate enough to enjoy an intimate acquaintance with him always find him generous and self-sacrificing to a fault, and will be glad to testify that they have never known a more delightful companion or truer sportsman, afield or afloat, than Mr. Carlin.

A. L. ARTMAN HIMMELWRIGHT was horn in Milford Square, Bucks County, Pa., February 7th, 1865. He early manifested a love for athletics and outdoor sports, and never was more delighted than when allowed to accompany his uncle, Mahlon Artman, of Philadelphia, who yearly took a shooting trip into the country north of Philadelphia. Mr. Himmelwright's tastes led him to adopt the profession of civil engineering, and in June, 1888, he was graduated from the Rensselaer Polytechnic Institute, of Troy, N. Y.

After a six-months' hunting trip in the Coeur d'Alene and St. Joe region, of Idaho, in company with Mr. Carlin, he associated himself with the Northern Pacific Railroad Company, and was engaged during the whole of the winter of 1888-89 in the location of a railway line from Coeur d'Alene City to Old Mission, Idaho, An idea of the character of this work and the hardship and exposure it involved may be formed from the fact that the engineering corps lived in tents all winter, sixteen to twenty miles from the nearest ranch, and subsisted principally on game. The snow varied from two to four feet deep, occasionally stopping the pack train for several days, but never interfering with the progress of the work, except for one day. In addition to the Northern Pacific Railroad, Mr. Himmelwright has been connected professionally with the Pennsylvania Railroad, and the Rome, Watertown, and Ogdensburg Railroad. The last four years he has been engaged in the design and construction of plants for industrial enterprises, notable among these being the elaborate plant of the Benvenue Granite Quarries, on the Connecticut River, near Middletown, Conn.

Mr. Himmelwright is a serious, busy man. Although quiet and reserved in manner and a slave to his profession, he can, when opportunity offers, enjoy a vacation, and is one of the kindest and most companionable persons imaginable in camp.

JOHN HARVEY PIERCE, Mr. Carlin's brother-in-law, was born in White Plains, N. Y., on July 28th, 1873. He has always been very fond of shooting, and had been on hunting trips in Tennessee and Florida previous to his experience in Idaho. He has acted in the capacity of assistant to his father – Dr. H. M. Pierce – in his varied business associations, and was for about a year connected with a business house in Buffalo, N. Y.

While in Florida, in 1892, on a cruise in the Gulf of Mexico south of Homosassa, with E. W. Agnew, Jr., of Ocala, he was taken violently ill with malarial fever, from the effects of which he had not entirely recovered at the time he went West in the fall of 1893 – the purpose of the trip being partly to improve his health. He was most fortunate in successfully passing through all the hardship and exposure incident to the trip without serious consequences.

MARTIN P. SPENCER, the guide of the party, was born in Manchester, Iowa, in 1866, and re-sided in Iowa until 1883. Being a sufferer from asthma, he left his native State and sought relief from his affliction in the higher altitudes of the Rocky Mountains, and finally took up his residence in Spokane, Wash. His fondness for hunting, as well the benefit he derived from trips into the mountains, led him to adopt the occupation of guide, which he has followed, more or less, for the past eight years. He is a careful, reliable man, and is what, in Western parlance, is called a " hustler." He knows the trails of the Clearwater Basin perfectly, and has sound ideas on all subjects relating to hunting and the woods. Thoroughly familiar with the habits of large game, and a successful hunter himself, he makes a capital guide, and a valuable companion in camp.

GEORGE COLGATE was born in Kent, England, in 1841, where he was brought up and educated. He subsequently removed to Liverpool, where he remained a number of years, and there connected himself with the London and Northwestern Railway, remaining in the employ of that company about ten years. He next accepted a position in the household of the Hon. William E. Gladstone, where he remained until his departure for this country, about seventeen years ago. He was next employed by A. E. Head, of San Francisco, but subsequently went into business for himself at Dayton, Wash. He removed to Idaho in 1887, where he owned and operated a large shingle-mill. He finally settled in Post Falls, where, soon after his arrival, he was elected justice of the peace, which office he held up to the time of his departure with the ill-fated hunting party. A wife and seven children survive him.

George Colgate had accompanied W. E. Carlin and A. L. A. Himmelwright on a former hunting trip up the St. Mary's River, in the Coeur d'Alene country of northern Idaho, in the spring of 1889. He was a strong, active man, an excellent cook, understood skinning animals and curing hides, and was a very handy man about camp. His work was so satisfactory on that occasion that when Mr. Carlin contemplated taking another trip in the Northwest, the first move was to write and engage Colgate. He met Mr. Carlin by appointment in Spokane on September 15th, 1893, to arrange the details of the proposed trip.

When Martin Spencer, the guide, saw him, he considered him too aged and feeble to undertake the trip, and recommended that he be left behind and a younger and more active man substituted for him. Mr. Carlin knew Colgate well, and while he differed with the guide on the point of Colgate's ability to stand the trip, in order to prevent any possible antagonism between the men, he endeavored to persuade Colgate to give up the trip and return home, offering to pay his expenses and a month's wages if he would do so. Colgate, however, declined to do this. Mr. Carlin then insisted that he consult his physician. Colgate soon after-ward returned, reporting that his physician had said that he could take the trip with safety. Feeling confident that Colgate was fully as able to withstand the fatigue of the trip as some of the other members of the party, Mr. Carlin decided he could go. No one knew of Colgate's trouble until he revealed it in camp, as stated elsewhere. Though he must have suffered severe pain from the time he left Kendrick (September 18th) to November 13th, when the rafts were abandoned, he never once complained of his own sufferings, but frequently expressed his regret that he was unable to attend to his duties, and that he was a burden to the party. His resolution and fortitude during the entire trip were most remarkable. Why he neglected to take his instruments, and why he concealed the fact that he did not have them until too late to remedy the oversight, will perhaps always remain a mystery, unless it can be explained by the effects of his long-standing ailment, which, in twenty years, may have impaired his faculties.

APPENDIX E.
A FEW HINTS RELATIVE TO SUITABLE ARMS FOR BIG-GAME SHOOTING

THE primary requisite of an arm for big-game shooting is accuracy, and any of our first-class rifles have sufficient accuracy for general hunting purposes. In hunting where very long shots are the rule, one must get a rifle and cartridge whose ballistic properties fit it for such work. Most large game is killed within one hundred yards, and one hundred and fifty yards is a good, long shot. We can no more expect one rifle to be suited to all kinds of shooting than we can expect any other machine to be adapted to all kinds of work. For such game as moose, elk, large bear, etc., the bullet should have a large diameter, good weight, and a fairly high velocity, in order that it may combine great shock and penetration.

The powder-charge and bullet should bear a relation to each other of 1 to 3.5, or 1 to 4.0, which would give in a .45-calibre rifle a bullet weighing, say, 405 grs., and from 100 to 120 grs. of powder; in a .50-calibre rifle, a bullet weighing 450 or 500 grs., and a powder-charge of 120 to 130 grs. The velocity should not be less than 1,500 ft. per sec., and from 1,600 to1,800 ft. per sec. would be better.

APPENDIX E.

One object should be to "smash" an animal down in its tracks, and this can only be accomplished by the application of great power. An ideal rifle for big and dangerous game is Messrs. Holland & Holland's .577 calibre, which shoots 164 grs. of good powder and a solid bullet of 598 grs. This charge combines every requisite for large - game shooting, including accuracy. No matter in what position an animal is standing, this charge has been found to slash its way through all opposing bone and muscle, and usually kills with one shot. Its weight, eleven pounds or over, prevents it from being used by many who prefer a lighter arm.

Another useful arm, and one that has given great satisfaction, is the combined ball and shot gun, originally patented under the name " Para-dox." In 12-bore, it need not weigh over eight pounds, and may be lighter. It shoots conical bullets with all necessary accuracy at 150 yards, and even farther. The bullets weigh from 530 to 750 grs. For big game, the bullets should weigh at least 600 or 650 grs., with a charge of 100 or 110 grs. of high-grade powder, such as Curtis & Harvey No. 6, or Hazzard's Ducking No. 4. This is not enough to produce a high velocity, but the low velocity is practically compensated for by the greater shock of the large, heavy bullet.

These are charges that, from long and varied use, have been found to kill well – not merely wound. We have but few cartridges in this country that are fit for use on large game. Most of our charges are moderately powerful only, and are good for deer shooting principally. They will kill big game when hit in the right place, but there is abundant evidence that they are, as might be expected, far from satisfactory when shooting big game in difficult positions, when a good deal of penetration is necessary to crush through bone and muscle. The .50-110-300 Winchester, for instance, has been recommended by some writers as most suitable for shooting musk-oxen and grizzly bears. It appears to be a very good cartridge for shooting deer, but nothing larger. There are many instances of its failure to kill big game, when fairly hit. The proper way to judge a rifle's merits is not by certain kills, but by the number of animals that are fairly hit and get away wounded. If this cartridge and rifle were remodelled to use a 450-gr. bullet and 110 to 120 grs. of first-rate powder, it might behave quite differently.

The .45-90 has been a popular rifle. The .45-90- 300 cartridge is a very fine deer charge, and the .45-82-405, which is used in the same rifle, is fairly satisfactory for larger game. The same may be said of the .45-70 and its various charges.

The fad for light recoil and low trajectory at short ranges in this country has caused, in the first place, the moderate charge; then, to get a lower curve and still not increase the recoil, the bullets have been lightened until rendered unfit for use on large or dangerous game.

Perhaps the greatest delusion entertained by many on the subject of charges is the light " ex-press," or hollow bullet, for use on large game, its wonderful effect, shock, etc.

The extreme popularity of the small-bore in this country is, no doubt, mostly due to the wonderful stories handed down (and, like a good liquor, improving with age) of the wonderful performances of our ancestors with the old Kentucky rifle, having a barrel as large as a crowbar and a bullet as small as a pea. No one appreciates the small-bore more than the writer, but it is out of its sphere of usefulness in big-game shooting. What may be done with the new high-power military rifle by using suitable compound bullets – with the nose of soft lead and the rest covered by a steel jacket – is as yet hard to say.

The recoil of fairly heavy charges need not be dreaded, if one holds the gun properly. It is evident that the gun has a motion backward, and must move over a certain distance unless a resistance sufficient to stop it is opposed to it. Now, if the gun be held loosely to the shoulder, it will move over the first part of its path with little resistance opposing it, and when it gets to the shoulder, it will deliver a blow rather than a steady push; on the other hand, if held very tightly against the shoulder a violent blow will again result, as the entire recoil is imparted directly to the shoulder, whereas it should he decreased by the energy used in first imparting motion to the gun. If held neither too tight nor too loose, the recoil will be a steady push. Just how tight it should be held to the shoulder to make the recoil felt the least, must be found out by trial.

On page 214 is a short table, which shows the ballistic properties of various charges, so that one may easily compare them.

CARTRIDGE.	Value of d²/w	VELOCITY OF THE BULLET IN FEET PER SECOND AT—					ENERGY OF THE BULLET IN FOOT-POUNDS AT—					TRAJECTORY.		ACCURACY. Diameter of the circle in inches that may ordinarily be expected to enclose the majority of the shots.		
		Muzzle.	50 yds.	100 yds.	150 yds.	200 yds.	Muzzle.	50 yds.	100 yds.	150 yds.	200 yds.	Height of bullet above horizontal plane at 75 yds., when shooting at 150 yds.	Height of bullet above horizontal plane at 100 yds., when shooting at 200 yds.	100 yds.	150 yds.	300 yds.
.45—70—350	5.000	1420	1274	1153	1057	996	1567	1261	1038	908	771	......	11.8 in.	3.0 in.	......	8 in.
.45—70—405	3.500	1325	1231	1150	1080	1028	1577	1359	1180	1049	950	......	11.9 in.	2.5 in.	......	6 in.
.45—90—300	4.728	1544	1390	1256	1144	1055	1589	1287	1050	871	741	......	11.0 in.	3.0 in.	......	8 in.
.50—110—300	5.833	1540	1354	1199	1076	999	1564	1221	957	771	664	......	11.5 in.	4.5 in.	......	20 in.
*.45—110—405	3.500	1480	1370	1270	1184	1109	1975	1692	1454	1264	1109	......	11.0 in.	3.0 in.	......	8 in.
.45—110—500	2.885	1425	1339	1260	1190	1128	2254	1980	1762	1571	1412	......	10.4 in.	3.0 in.	......	8 in.
†.50—188—444	3.941	1754	1641	1506	1379	1267	3137	2854	2381	1874	1580	4.7 in.	......	3.0 in.	7 in.	......
†.57—164—600	8.790	1663	1532	1408	1297	1200	3684	3127	2641	2241	1918	4.8 in.	......	6.0 in.	8 in.	......
12-bore "paradox," 110 grains powder, C. & H. No. 6, and 650-grain solid bullet	5.735	1200	1079	1002	942	889	2077	1679	1448	1280	1166	10 in.‡	19 in.‡	5.0 in.	......	12 in.

* Curtis & Harvey powder No. 6.
† Data for these charges were given by two double rifles by Holland & Holland.
‡ Calculated heights.

The height of the various bullets, except that of the paradox, above the horizontal plane at 50 yards, when shooting 100 yards, will be from about 2 inches to 2.6 inches, and for the paradox about 3.8 inches.

In the second column, d=diameter of bullet in inches; w=weight of bullet in pounds.

APPENDIX F.
SOME PRESS ACCOUNTS

The following account was published in one of the prominent daily newspapers of the Pacific Slope, under date of November 26th:

CARLIN'S PARTY FOUND

Destitute and Crazed With Suffering.

Abandonment of the Cook Necessitated.

He Became Weak, and to Save Themselves the Others Left Him to Die.

Special Dispatch to the CHRONICLE.

MISSOULA (Mont.), November 25.—Greatly to the surprise of every one the Carlin party, consisting of Will T. Carlin, W. H. Himmelwright and J. Harvey Pierce, the young New Yorkers who have been be-

IN THE HEART OF THE BITTER-ROOT MOUNTAINS:
The Story of "the Carlin Hunting Party"

sieged in Bitter Root mountains, southwest of this point, for nearly two months, has been found more dead than alive.

The account of their sufferings, as related by a courier just arrived, is harrowing in the extreme. The joy of the men at their release must be witnessed to be appreciated.

The courier arrived at 5 o'clock this morning, having ridden more than 100 miles, bearing the announcement that the party, except Cook & Colgate, had been found by Lieutenant Elliott's relief corps on the middle fork of the Clearwater, 130 miles from any habitation.

They were famished, without horses or provisions, barefooted, only the soles of their shoes remaining, and were scant of clothing.

Hemmed in by impenetrable snow banks and after several ineffectual attempts to escape, the party became resigned to its fate, trusting to Providence for relief. Another thirty-six hours would have frozen them.

Lieutenant Elliott found the men in a condition verging on insanity. He administered what immediate relief was at his command. Colgate, he learned, was still behind, having fallen in his inability to keep up with the party. This necessitated in Elliot's sending back for additional relief to search for Colgate, though Carlin believes that it is too late and that the man will not be found alive.

When the men were found they were totally bewildered and were wandering about aimlessly on a snow-covered plateau on which the depth of snow averaged fourteen feet. Their horses had long since stampeded and their provisions were exhausted, save what little they carried in their pockets. When the men were found they were slowly making their way down the river on a raft.

The courier gives the following account of their experiences in the mountains, dating from the time that they discovered that they were irretrievably lost, unless heroic methods were at once adopted to make their way out of the wilderness:

On the 5th of October, the day upon which they were preparing to leave the Clearwater, a heavy storm came on which completely obliterated all the roads and trails. To add to their distress their animals stampeded and when night overtook them they were powerless to proceed, being without snow shoes or other appliances for winter traveling.

Their perilous situation was soon realized and it at once became apparent that the party was in for it. That night there fell more than five feet of snow and the following morning the outlook was indeed cheerless.

Consultations were held, but no definite plan of action was decided upon until the following evening, when Guide Spencer decided upon braving the storm alone, promising to go to a certain point he had in view, which, if he could reach with safety, all would be well.

This, however, he failed to do, the remainder of the party not consenting, preferring that all should live or die together. So the little band remained, trusting to fate and awaiting succor, which arrived nearly too late.

The little band of brave men were making their last and final effort to get out when found, and thirty-six hours later would have found them dead. The cook, George Colgate, gave out a few days before the rescue and was left to perish, as it was feared that all would suffer the same fate if they should remain with him. The story of their hardships is indescribable.

As soon as Mr. Elliott reached the men and provided them with everything possible to make them comfortable they organized a party to go back and rescue Colgate, the cook, dead or alive. It is stated that the leaving of Colgate behind was a most heartrending scene, but as it was a case of life or death to those who remained the abandonment of the man was inevitable.

Lieutenant Elliott went as far as he could with horses. He then borrowed a

IN THE HEART OF THE

> saw at a rancher's cabin, made a skiff, and had gone up the river in it thirteen miles when he met the party.
>
> The Elliott relief party was fitted out in Spokane by Captain Merriam two weeks ago, going into the Bitter Root mountains by way of Kendrick, Idaho.
>
> The rescued and rescuers are expected to arrive at Kendrick on Monday or Tuesday of next week. They are still a long distance from that point and many hardships will yet have to be encountered before the rescue can be termed complete.

A leading Chicago newspaper delighted its readers with the following account of the rescue, on the morning of November 26th:

RESCUED FROM DEATH

CARLIN HUNTING PARTY IS FOUND.

Relief Expedition Comes Upon the Lost Hunters 130 Miles From Civilization.
—Without Food and Clothing—
One Man Still Missing.

SPOKANE, Wash., Nov. 25.—A courier arrived here at 5 o'clock this morning, after an all night ride from Weippe, with the news that Lieutenant Elliott had found the Carlin party in the Middle Fork of the

Clear Water, 130 miles from the nearest town, last Wednesday. The lost party consisted of W. E. Carlin, J. H. Pierce, A. H. Himmelwright and M. Spencer, guide. They were in bad shape when found, being out of provisions, nearly starved, and barefoot and with scarcely any clothing. They were slowly making their way down the river. George Colgate, the cook of the party, gave out a few days before the rescue and had to be left and it is feared may have died. All possible will be done to find him dead or alive. The rescued and the rescuers are expected here on Tuesday and General Carlin will meet the party here.

The story of suffering, desperation and hardship told by the lost hunters was frightful. Ever since the heavy snows set in, in the Bitter Root mountains, they told Lieutenant Elliott, they had been making an effort to return to Kendrick, and they knew it would take all the will and perseverance of desperate men to keep them from perishing of cold, fatigue and hunger. For many days they had battled with the mountain blasts and drifting snow, slowly beating their way down the clear water in an effort to reach civilization. Their progress was impeded by the swollen river, which was often blocked with floating ice, rendering passage exceedingly difficult and dangerous. They managed to cross the clear water in several places at great risk to their lives, being compelled to wade the icy current up to their necks or swim amid the floating blocks of ice and snow. Nearly all the horses died of cold and starvation.

Fought Against Death.

The suffering of the men was intense. They tramped for miles through the deep snow in blinding storms with scarcely any food or clothing. The food supply, it was seen from the first, would have to be jealously guarded or else it would be exhausted, and starvation would be the result in the event that game could not be had, which seemed to be quite probable. The men were put on half rations of bacon and bread. Their shoes had become worn out from constant tramping over the mountain rocks and their clothing was torn into shreds. At last the struggle became too much for George Colgate, the cook of the party. He became utterly exhausted and was unable to proceed further. Colgate realized the situation fully and advised his companions to attempt to save themselves.

It began to appear as if all would be lost, and almost the only hope held out to them was the chance of being found by a relief party which Carlin said he felt sure would be sent out to find them. The progress through the snow was very slow owing to the exhausted condition of the men and the extreme cold. But they pushed ahead with the spirit of desperation, determined to work for their deliverance so long as they were able to move.

Rescuers Warmly Welcomed.

When Lieutenant Elliott and his brave and sturdy snowshoers came upon the exhausted men in the middle fork of the Clear Water they were bravely fighting their way through the snow, but the reception they gave the gallant officer and his men was more than a welcome. Men who for weeks had been struggling almost against hope knew they were saved and they wept for joy. They were given plenty of food, some clothing, and, after a rest, the Elliott party proceeded on to where Colgate was left, with the hope of saving him if possible.

Mr. Carlin, in speaking of their experience, said that they had enjoyed excellent sport up to within four weeks ago, when snow began falling and continued almost constantly. About three weeks ago, during a lull in the storm, the party broke camp for a moose hunt. At the head of Clear Water River a fierce snowstorm and blizzard again set in and they soon realized that they were lost. Then began a fearful struggle between them and death. The snow soon became so deep that their horses became worthless and were abandoned. For days they struggled and floundered through snow seeking to recover the lost trail. The snow becoming deeper and deeper they were obliged to discard all baggage and part of their provisions, even some of their outer garments. Later they began to suffer torture from cold and hunger and their shoes became worn through. They bundled their feet as best they could. They were in despair of ever getting out alive and could not have survived much longer.

Over Two Months.

The Carlin party has been out since Sept. 15 and the Elliott relief party was fitted out in Spokane by Captain Merriam two weeks ago, and left for the Bitter Root Mountains by way of Kendrick, Idaho, having been two weeks in reaching the lost hunters. Captain Merriam, who has been waiting in Spokane with the intention of fitting out another party of snowshoers and taking command himself should those that are out fail, received the following telegram:

TO CAPTAIN MERRIAM:—Lieutenant Elliott found the lost party on the 22d. All well except Colgate, who is not yet found. Recall all searchers.   W. P. CARLIN.

Captain Merriam was seen this evening. His voice was not steady, and two big tears came into his eyes when he was asked about the lost party. "Yes, I know that country well," he said, "and it seems as if some higher power must have given the poor boy and his associates greater strength. It is one of the hardest countries to get over in the world. Just think of it, and no provisions either. It is a wonder to me that they are not all dead, but I think it would have killed General Carlin to have learned that his son was dead. The general will meet the party in Spokane next Monday night or Tuesday."

IN THE HEART OF THE BITTER-ROOT MOUNTAINS:
The Story of "the Carlin Hunting Party"

A sensational New York daily newspaper produced the following, on December 16th:

GEORGE COLGATE FOUND.

He Bitterly Denounces the Carlin Party for Deserting Him.

(Special to The World.)

MISSOULA, Mon., Dec. 15.—It is reported here to-day that George Colgate, who was the cook for the Carlin party which narrowly escaped death in the hills, has been found. John Mack, a railroad brakeman on the Northern Pacific road, is responsible for the story.

Mack says that Colgate was found by two trappers wandering through the mountains in a heavy snowstorm and almost dead. They took him to a cabin they had erected, and later to Lewiston, where he is now being cared for.

Mack says that Colgate was bitter in his denunciations of the other members of the Carlin party, who, he said, left him to starve and freeze to death.

He says they deserted him because he was unable to walk any longer. After he had rested he started to follow the party, got lost and wandered about the mountains for three weeks with scarcely anything to eat and no shelter. Then he was found by the two trappers.

The other members of the Carlin party are not inclined to believe the story, and insist that when they left Colgate he was barely alive and could live but a few hours.

Trapper Keely denounces the action of the Carlin party as most inhuman. He says that he wished to leave Colgate some food, but they would not permit it, saying that they had purchased the eatables and had not enough for themselves.

Trapper Keely is suing Gen. Cathn for the reward for finding the party.

APPENDIX G.
LEWIS AND CLARK'S JOURNEY THROUGH THE CLEARWATER COUNTRY

Note.- The Lewis and Clark Expedition has been appropriately termed – "our national epic of exploration." That a small band of twenty-nine men should hazard a journey of one-third the circumference of the globe, through an unknown region inhabited solely by Indians often at war with each other; cut themselves off from all communication with the civilized world for a period of sixteen months, during which time they were compelled to rely on the unknown resources of the wild region they were traversing for subsistence; successfully surmount every obstacle in their path; overcome every difficulty that menaced them; disregard hardship, suffering, peril, and sickness; and undiscouraged, resolute, invincible, push on to a fruitful and successful consummation of their labors, stamps this as the most daring, brilliant and unparalleled achievement of modern times, and speaks more than volumes for the genius, foresight, tact, and remarkable ability of the leader- Lewis and Clark.

The Lewis and Clark Expedition – to the Pacific Ocean was made in 1803-6 Under the direction and auspices of the United States Goverment. The idea was conceived by Thomas Jefferson, then President of the United States, soon after the acquisition of the Louisiana Territory (April 30th, 1803), the purpose or the expedition being " to discover the courses and sources of the Missouri and the most convenient water communication thence to the Pacific Ocean."

IN THE HEART OF THE BITTER-ROOT MOUNTAINS:
The Story of "the Carlin Hunting Party"

President Jefferson's private secretary, Capt. Meriwether Lewis, and Capt William Clark both officers of the United States Army, were associated in the command of this enterprise. The party consisted of the two officers named, nine young men from Kentucky, fourteen soldiers of the United States Army, who had volunteered their services two boatmen, one interpreter who acted also in the capacity of hunter, and a black servant belonging to Captain Clark. Having devoted the greater part of the preceding year in preparing, collecting, and arranging equipment, the party started from St.Louis, then the most remote Western settlement and a mere village, on May 14th 1804. Their course lay up the Missouri River to its headwaters, thence across the Bitter-Root Mountains, descending the Clearwater, Snake, and Columbia Rivers, respectively, to the Pacific Ocean.

The winter of 1804-6 was spent at Fort Mandan, near the present town of that name. After ascending the Missouri to its head, a number of auxiliary trips were made during the summer, resulting in a very thorough exploration of that region and the passes of the mountains west of it. In September 1806, the journey to the Pacific Ocean was resumed, crossing the Bitter-Root Mountains at Lo-Lo Pass.

From this point the interesting: details of Lewis and Clark's journey westward through the Clearwater country are reproduced, almost in toto% as follows:

A REPRINT OF PORTIONS OF VOLS. II. AND III.
OF THE HISTORY OF THE LEWIS AND CLARK EXPEDITION.
EDITED BY ELLIOTT COUES.
[FRANCIS P. HARPER, NEW YORK, 1893.]

September 13th, 1805. – Two horses strayed away during the night, and one of them being Captain Lewis', he remained with four men to search for them, while we proceeded up the creek [Travelers' -rest]. At the distance of two miles we came to several springs issuing from large rocks of a coarse, hard grit, and nearly boiling hot. These seemed to be much frequented, as there are several paths made by elk, deer, and other animals, near one of the springs a hole or Indian bath, and roads leading in different directions. These embarrassed our guide, who, mistaking the road, took us three miles out of the proper course over an exceedingly bad route. We then fell into the right road, and proceeded on very well, till, having made five miles, we stopped to refresh the horses. Captain Lewis here joined us; but not having been able to find his horse, two men were sent back to continue the search. We then proceeded along the same kind of country which we passed yesterday, and after crossing a mountain* and

---

* "Thus crossing the main divide of the Bitter-Root Mountains, from the Missoula watershed on the east to the basin of the Kookooskee or Clearwater on the west, and so passing. over from Montana into Idaho (Shoshone County). This "new creek" which the expedition strikes and calls Glade creek., is one of the headwaters of the Kooskooskee or Clearwater River The party at this point is nearly due east of Pierce City. The mountain they have passed is at least 7,000 feet high. The pass just now made is known as the Lo-Lo Pass, from the creek which the expedition has ascended. Hence the route is to-be from east to west, right across Idaho, to the main forks of the Kooskooskee; and thence, by canoes built there, down to Lewiston at the junction of the Kooskooskee with the Snake, thus finishing with Idaho. and reaching Washington. The land journey is 150 miles [roundly] As already intimated, the track of the expedition is approximately the-old northern Nez Perces trail, also called the Lo-Lo trail. It is approximately the Mullan trail of September, 1854, as charted on Stevens' map. It likewise approaches to some extent the southern border of Shoshone County. But with half a dozen of the best modern maps of Idaho before me there is not one on which I can dot the trail of the expedition in detail. The country has not yet been sectionized, and our topographical knowledge is still too vague to be of any exact use. I propose to follow Lewis and Clark's footsteps

leaving the Sources of Travelers' rest Creek on the left, reached, after five miles' riding, a small creek which came in from the left hand, passing through open glades, some of which were half a mile wide. The road, which had been as usual rugged and stony, became firm, plain, and level after quitting the head of Travelers' -rest. We followed [down] the course of this new [Glade] creek for two miles, and camped* at a spot where the mountains close in on each side. Other mountains, covered with snow, are in view to the southeast and southwest. We were somewhat more fortunate to-day in killing a deer, and several pheasants, which were of the common species, except that the tail was black.

September 14th. – The day was very cloudy with rain and hail in the valley, while on top of the mountains some

---

across these mountains. They were never spirited. from one point to any other: they stepped off every foot of the way Clark's detailed courses and distances have never before been published. I give them complete. If the ascribed distances do not suit modern measurements, that is no affair of mine. If the creeks run the wrong way on paper, they run the right way on the ground that Lewis and Clark went over, and the maps can be reconstructed, upon determination of the correction of Clark's compass-courses required for the magnetic variation.

* September 13th, Clark G. 130: "S. W. two miles up the said [Traveler's-rest] creek bad road rockey steep hillsides falling timber to hot springs on the right of the creek boiling out of a corse grittey stones, &c. S. 80° W. three miles passing a bad falling timber to the creek on our left passed three small streams from our right. S. 30° W. seven-miles over a mountain and on a dividing [plateau now known as Summit Prairie] of flat gladey land to a [Glade] creek in a glade. of one half a mile in width, & keeping down this creek two miles " So from the. fixed. point of the hot springs, the course is straight for ten miles S 30° W to a point on Glade creek, which creek comes from the left or east, and is flowing westwardly.

APPENDIX G.

snow fell. We proceeded early, continuing along the right side of Glade Creek, crossed a high [about 7, 000 feet] mountain, and at the distance of six miles reached the place where it [Glade Creek] is joined by another branch of equal size from the right [thus composing the Kooskooskee river]. Near these forks the Tushepaws have had a camp, which is but recently abandoned, for the grass is entirely destroyed by horses, and two fish-weirs across the creek are still remaining; no fish were, however, to be seen. We here passed over the left side of the [Glade] creek, and began the ascent of a very high and steep mountain, nine miles across. On reaching the other side we found a large branch [Colt-killed, of the Kooskooskee] from the left, which seems to rise in the snowy mountains to the south and southeast. We [crossed the main stream, Clark G. 111, and] continued along the creek [*i.e.*, down right bank of the Kooskooskee] two miles farther, when, night coming on, we camped* opposite a small island, at the mouth of a branch [which fell in] on the right side of the [Kooskooskee] river. The mountains which we crossed

---

* September 14, Clark G. 131: "S. 80° W. six miles over a high mountainous country thickly covered with pine, spruce, &c., to the forks of the creek, one of equal size falling in from the right, passing much falling timber. S. 60° W., over a high mountain steep and almost in excessable leaving the creek to our right hand to the forks, a [Colt-killed] creek of equal size falling in from the left two fish dams or weares across the north [Kooskooskee] fork to catch salmon. S. 70° W. two miles down the river Kooskooske to a small branch on the right side killed and eate coalt." Thus seventeen miles, much of it "in the air" over two mountains to a point on the supposed Kooskooskee River, two miles below a considerable branch from the south; camp on right bank of the river, at mouth of an unnamed creek from the north (Codex has a crossing not given by Biddle).

to-day were much more difficult than those of yesterday; the last was particularly fatiguing, being steep and stony, broken by fallen timber, and thickly overgrown by pine, spruce, fir, hackmatack, and tamarack. Although we had made only seventeen miles, we were all very weary. The whole stock of animal food being now exhausted, we therefore killed a colt, on which we made a hearty supper. From this incident we called the last creek we had passed [coming], from the south, Colt-killed Creek. The river itself is eighty yards wide, with a swift current and a stony channel. Its Indian name is Kooskooskee.*

Sunday, September 15th. – At an early hour we proceeded along the right side of the Kooskooskee, over steep, rocky points of land, till at the distance of four miles we reached an old Indian fishing-place. The road here turned to the right of the water, and began to ascend a mountain. But the fire and wind had prostrated or dried almost all the timber on the south side, and the ascents were so steep that we were forced to wind in every direction round the high knobs, which constantly impeded

---

* This name variable as usual in spelling; c or k in one, two, or three places; single or double o and s; ending ee, e, i, ie, ia; the syllables sometimes hyphenated, or separated. It will frequently recur as the narrative proceeds, and its application will vary as the expedition learns more of the geography of the unknown region now being- explored. "Kooskooskee" is the Indian name of the river now called the Clearwater, rising in the Bitter -Root Mountains, draining the-country west of these mountains and north of the Salmon River water. shed, and falling into the Snake at county town of Lewiston Nez Perces County, a little west of Fort Lapwai. Under date of October 7th, it is said that the Kooskooskee is only so called downward from " its forks," i.e., where the main north fork of the Clearwater falls in. But this is immaterial, for "Clearwater" is now the name. of the mainstream to its proper head in the Bitter-Root Mountains.

APPENDIX G.

our progress. Several of the horses lost their foothold and slipped; one of them, which was loaded with a desk and small trunk, rolled over and over for 40 yards, till his fall was stopped by a tree. The desk was broken, but the poor animal escaped without much injury. After clambering in this way for four miles, we came to a high, snowy part of the mountains, where was a spring of water, at which we halted two hours to re-fresh our horses.

On leaving this spring, this road continued as bad as it was below, and the timber more abundant. At four miles we reached the top of the mountain; foreseeing no chance of meeting with water, we camped* on the northern side of this mountain, near an old bank of snow three feet deep. Some of this we melted, and supped on the remains of the colt killed yesterday. Our only game today was two pheasants; the horses, on which we calculated as a last resource, began to fail us* for two of them were so poor and worn out with fatigue that we were obliged to leave them behind. All around us are high, rugged mountains, among which is a lofty range from southeast to northwest, whose tops are without timber, and in some places covered with snow. The night was cloudy and very cold.

September 16th. Three hours before daybreak, it began to snow and continued all day, so that by evening it

---

* September 15th, Clark G. 131: " West four miles down the river, passing over four high steep hills to a run at old Indn. encampment. N. W. eight miles ascending a ruged mountain winding in every direction passing over high stoney knobs, passed a spring on our right. at four miles to a high part of the mountain on which was snow " Note this northwest. course, away from the river; camp also on north side of mountain Most of the way was zigzag as well as in the air, and actual advance. may not have been over six or eight miles for the twelve travelled.

IN THE HEART OF THE BITTER-ROOT MOUNTAINS:
The Story of "the Carlin Hunting Party"

was six or eight inches deep. This covered the track so completely that we were obliged constantly to halt and examine, lest we should lose the route. In many places we had nothing to guide us except the branches of the trees, which being low, had been rubbed by the burdens of the Indian horses. The road was like that of yesterday, along steep hill-sides, obstructed with fallen timber and a growth of eight different species of pine, so thickly strewed that the snow fell from them as we passed; this kept us continually wet to the skin, and so cold that we were anxious lest our feet should be frozen, as we had only thin moccasins to defend them.

At noon we halted to let the horses feed on some long grass on the south side of the mountain, and endeavored by making fires to keep ourselves warm. As soon as the horses were refreshed, Captain Clark went ahead with one man, at the distance of six miles reached a stream* from [the left to] the right, and prepared fires by the time of our arrival at dusk. We here camped in a piece of loground thickly timbered, but scarcely large enough to permit us to lie level. We had now made thirteen miles.

---

* Worst possible snag in this stream, "from the right." Read from the left to the right: " A small branch passing to the right, " Clark G. 114, September 16th; and again, Clark G. 182, September 16th: "S. 75° W. 13 miles on the mountain passing emmencely high ruged knobs of the mounts in snow from four to six inches deep, much falling timber, snow continued to fall passed thro a countery thickly timbered with eight destunct kinds of pine to a small branch passing to our right. Perhaps no passage in this itinerary has done more to " throw off " the L. and C. trail than this unlucky slip. The expedition at this point is away from the main Kooskooskee altogether, a mountain intervening. and has struck on a creek flowing northward. It is, therefore, a separate watershed from that of the main Kooskooskee basin. See itinerary of June 27th.

We were all very wet, cold, and hungry. Though before setting out this morning we had seen four deer, yet we could not procure any of them, and were obliged to kill a second colt for our supper.

September 17th. Our horses became so much scattered during the night that we were detained till one o'clock before they were all collected. We then continued our route over high, rough knobs,* 89 and several drains and springs, along a ridge of country separating the waters of two small rivers. The road was still difficult; several of the horses fell and injured themselves very much, so that we were unable to advance more than ten miles to a small stream [running southward, to our left], on which we camped.

We had killed a few pheasants; but these being insufficient for our subsistence, we killed another of the colts. This want of provisions, the extreme fatigue to which we were subjected, and the dreary prospects before us, began to dispirit the men. It was therefore agreed that Captain Clark should go on ahead with six hunters, and endeavor to kill something for – the support of the party.

---

* September 17th, Clark G. 132: "S. 50° W. 10 miles over high knobs of the moumtn. immencely dificuelt, passed 3 dreans [drains] to our right [and came to] one which passes to our left on the top of a high mountain, passing on [going along] a dividing ridge." This is nearly a southwest course, and with more actual advance for the miles traveled than yesterday and the day before that, as it is along a dividing ridge: it takes them past several runs to the north, and brings them to a camp at a run to the south. They – have therefore crossed a divide,-and. are again on a southern watershed not that of the main Kooskoos kee but of. its tributary, the Lo-Lo fork, otherwise known as the Nah-wah River.

IN THE HEART OF THE BITTER-ROOT MOUNTAINS:
The Story of "the Carlin Hunting Party"

September 18th. He therefore set out,* 30 early in the morning, in hopes of finding a level country, from which he might send back some game. His route lay S. 85° W., along the same high dividing ridge, and the road was still very bad, but he moved on rapidly, and at the distance of twenty miles was rejoiced on discovering far off an extensive plain toward the west and southwest, bounded by a high mountain. He halted an hour to let the horses eat a little grass on the hill-sides, and then went on twelve and a half miles till he reached a bold creek, running to the left, on which he camped. To this stream he gave the very appropriate name of Hungry** Creek; for, having procured no game, the party had nothing to eat.

In the mean time we were detained till after eight o'clock by the loss of one of our horses, which had strayed away and could not be found. We then proceeded, but having soon finished the remainder of the colt killed yesterday, felt the want of provisions; which was more sensible from our meeting with no water till, toward nightfall, we found some in a ravine among the hills. By pushing

---

* Two parallel narratives continue hence to September 23d. The situation was grave: "A coalt being – the most useless part of our stock, he fell a Prey to our appetites." Clark G. 116 .

** "A bold running creek passing to the left – which I call Hungery creek as at that place we had nothing to eat." Clark G. 117. "S. 85° W. 32 miles to Hungary creek passing to our left, passed a branch & several springs – which passes to our right, keeping a dividing ridge, " etc. Clark G. 132. This- long course, nearly west, is on the divide between the waters of Lo-Lo fork or Nahwah River on the south,-and other tributaries of the Kooskooskee system to the north; as Hungry creek runs to the left, southward, it is supposably a branch of the former river; on which supposition it maybe identifiable. with the Mussel shell creek of present maps, or branch of this.

our horses to their utmost strength, we made eighteen miles. We then melted some snow, and supped on a little portable soup, a few canisters of which, with about twenty [pounds] weight of bear's oil, are our only remaining means of subsistence. Our guns are scarcely of any service, for there is no living creature in these mountains, except a few pheasants, a small species of gray squirrel, and a blue bird of the vulture kind* about the size of a turtle-dove or jay; even these are difficult to shoot.

September 19th. Captain the [Hungry] creek, along which the road was more steep and stony than any he had yet passed. At six miles distance, he reached a small plain, where he fortunately found a horse, on which he breakfasted, and hung the rest on a tree for the party in the rear. Two miles beyond this he left the creek [to his right] and crossed three high mountains, rendered almost impassable from the steepness of the ascent and the quantity of fallen timber. After clambering over these ridges and mountains, and passing the heads of some branches of Hungry Creek, he came to a large [Collins'] creek running westward [passing to our left, Clark G. 117]. This he followed for four miles, and then turned to the right down the mountain, till he came to a small creek [running] to the left. Here he halted, having made twenty-two miles on his course, S. 80° W., though the winding route over the mountains almost doubled the distance.**

---

* Meaning probably *Gymnokitta cyanocephala*; the squirrel. is *Sciurus fremonti*, a Western variety of the common squirrel, *S hudsonius*.

** Clark G. 132, September 19th: "S. 80° W. 22 miles on our course thro emencely bad falling timber the greater part of the way. Keeping up the [Hungry] creek for eight miles, at six passed thro

IN THE HEART OF THE BITTER-ROOT MOUNTAINS:
The Story of "the Carlin Hunting Party"

On descending the last mountain, the heat became much more sensible, after the extreme cold he had experienced for several days past. Besides the breakfast in the morning, two pheasants were their only food during the day. The only [other] kinds of birds they saw were the blue-jay [*Cyanocitta stelleri*], a small white-headed hawk [?], a larger hawk, crows, and ravens.

We followed soon after sunrise. At six miles the ridge terminated, and we had before us the cheering prospect of the large plain to the southwest. On leaving the ridge we again ascended and went down several mountains; six miles farther we came to Hungry Creek, where it was fifteen yards wide, and received the waters of a branch from

---

a small plain where we killed a horse, the road up the creek, stoney hill sides much worse than any we have passed, left the creek to our right and passd. over a mountain and the heads of some branches of Hungary creek, over ridges thro much falling timber & two other high mountains of like description to a large [Collins] creek running west, kept down [this creek] four miles, and left it to our left and crossed over a mountain as bad as usual to a branch which runs to our left. " This steady westward course which Captain Clark is holding does not agree at all with the meanders of this part of the 1854 Mullan trail as dotted on the Stevens map, which fetches out much farther south, by Kamai or Komeyer creek [Commearp creek of our text of May and June, 1806, now known as Lawyer's Canyon creek], and thus south of the Lo-Lo fork. Observe how nearly Captain Clark holds to west his southings are mostly 20° or less; and I believe the simple curved which you see on his 1814 map, as representing lines the L. and C. trail on a very small scale, is the most nearly accurate delineation we have of this "Lo-Lo" route. It is true that he runs Hungry creek due south into the Kooskooskee itself, and therefore cuts Collins creek down to a short westward run; but that does not obscure his route. This Collins creek is what is now called the Nahwah River, or Lo-Lo fork of the Kooskooskee; and Hungry creek is one of its northern tributaries. Clark is all right, as usual; next lap will fetch him out of the mountains and we can turn to our modern maps again.

the north. We went up it on a course nearly due west, and at three miles crossed a second branch flowing from the same quarter. The country is thickly covered with pine timber, of which we have enumerated eight distinct species. Three miles beyond this last branch of Hungry Creek we camped, after a fatiguing route of eighteen miles.

The road along the creek is a narrow rocky path near the borders of very high precipices, from which a fall seems almost inevitable destruction. One of our horses slipped and rolled over with his load down the hill-side, which was nearly perpendicular and strewed with large irregular rocks, nearly a hundred yards, and did not stop till he fell into the creek. We all expected he was killed; but to our astonishment, on taking off his load he rose, seemed but little injured, and in twenty minutes proceeded with his load. Having no other provisions, we took some portable soup, our only refreshment during the day. This abstinence, joined with fatigue, has a visible effect on our health. The men are growing weak and losing their flesh very fast; several are afflicted with dysentery, and eruptions of the skin are very common.

September 20th.[*] – Captain Clark went on through a

---

[*] Clark G. 133, September 20th: "S. 60° W. 12 miles to the low countery at the foot of the mountain, passed over into the forks of a large creek at four miles. Kept down this creek two miles and left it to our left hand, passing on a dividing ridge, passed some dreans [drains] to our left. West six miles to an Pierced nose Indian village in a-small plain passed thro an open pine countery, crossed two runs pass ing to our left. N. 70° W. two miles to a second village passing through the open plains covered with horses, &c., & Indian womin diging roots. " Total twenty miles, little south of west on the whole. I understand that Captain Clark comes out on the Weippe prairie, north of the Nahwah River or Lo-Lo fork, in the vicinity or the present

country as rugged as usual, till, on passing a low mountain, he came at the distance of four miles to the forks of a large creek. Down this he kept on a course S. 60 W. for two miles; then, turning to the right, continued over a dividing ridge, where were the heads of several small streams, and at twelve miles' [total] distance descended the last of the Rocky mountains [Bitter-Root ranges] and reached the level country. A beautiful open plain, partially supplied with pine, now presented itself. He continued for five miles, when he discovered three Indian boys who, on observing the party, ran off and hid themselves in the grass. Captain Clark immediately alighted, and giving his horse and gun to one of the men, went after the boys. He soon relieved their apprehensions, and sent them forward to a village about a mile off, with presents of small pieces of ribbon.

Soon after the boys reached home, a man came out to meet the party, with great caution; but he conducted them to a large tent in the village, and all the inhabitants gathered round to view with a mixture of fear and pleasure these wonderful strangers. The conductor now informed Captain Clark, by signs, that the spacious tent was the residence of the great chief, who had set out three days ago with all the warriors to attack some of their enemies toward the southwest; that he would not return before fifteen or eighteen days, and that in the mean time

---

town of Weippe, and keeps on to a point some twelve or fifteen miles above the mouth of the creek now called Flores or Jim Ford's, which he will call Village creek, and which runs into the Kooskooskee from the east. He is still in Shoshone County, and is approaching the eastern-border of the present Nez Perces Indian reservation. This. low country is plainly lettered "Quamash Flats" on his map of 1814.

there were only a few men left to guard the women and children. They now set before them a small piece of buffalo-meat, some dried salmon, berries, and several kinds of roots. Among these last is one which is round, much like an onion in appearance, and sweet to the taste. It is called quamash, and is eaten either in its natural state, or boiled into a kind of soup, or made into a cake, which is then called pasheco.* After the long abstinence, this was a sumptuous treat. They returned the kindness of the people by a few small presents, and then went on in company with one of the chiefs to a second village in the same plain, at the distance of two miles. Here the party were treated with great kindness, and passed the night. The hunters were sent out, but, though they saw some tracks of deer, were not able to procure anything.

We were detained till ten o'clock before we could collect our scattered horses; we then proceeded for two miles, when, to our great joy, we found the horse which Captain Clark had killed; also a note apprising us of his intention of going to the plains toward the southwest, and collecting provisions by the time we reached him. At one o'clock we halted on a small stream, and made a hearty meal of

---

* "Quawmash or passhico," Clark G. 119, and in great profusion of spellings in the codices, *passim*; as for the former word, quamas, kamash, kamas, camash, camas, commas, etc., for the latter, pashequaw, pashequa, etc. The usual spellings are now camas or kamas and camass: from the latter form is the new Latin generic name *camassia*. This is applied to a genus of bulbous liliaceous plants of North America, nearly related to *Scilla* [squill], with long linear leaves and a scape with blue flowers in a raceme. The name is Indian. The are two Western species C. *esculenta* and C. *leichlini* growing in moist meadows from California to British Columbia Montana. Our text will have much to say of and these important food-plants.

IN THE HEART OF THE BITTER-ROOT MOUNTAINS:
The Story of "the Carlin Hunting Party"

horseflesh. On examination, it now appeared that one of the horses was missing, and the had been was directed to return man in whose charge he and search for him. He came back in about two hours without having been able to find the horse; but as the load was too valuable to be lost, two of the best woodsmen were directed to continue the search, while we proceeded. Our general course was S. 25° W.*, through a thick forest of large pine, which has fallen in many places and very much obstructs the road. After making about fifteen miles we camped on a ridge, where we could find but little grass and no water. We succeeded, however, in procuring some from a distance, and supped on the remainder of the horse.

On descending the heights of the mountains the soil becomes gradually more fertile, and the land through which we passed this evening is of an excellent quality. It has a dark gray soil, though it is very much broken, with large masses of gray freestone above the ground in many places. Among the vegetable productions we distinguished the alder [*Alnus incana?*], honeysuckle, and huckleberry [like those which are] common in the United States, and a species of honeysuckle known only westward of the Rocky Mountains, which rises to the height of about four feet and bears a white berry. There is also a plant resembling the choke cherry, which grows in thick clumps eight or ten feet high, and bears a black berry with a single stone, and of a sweetish taste. The arbor vitae [*Thuja occidentalis?*] is very common and grows to a great size, being from two to six feet in diameter.

---

*   Sic – but read S. 85° W. See Clark's course of September 18th. The expedition is on his trail.

APPENDIX G.

Saturday, September 21st. The free use of food, to which he had not been accustomed, made Captain Clark very sick* both yesterday evening and during the whole of today. He therefore sent out all the hunters and remained himself at the village, as well on account of his sickness, as for the purpose of avoiding suspicion and collecting information from the Indians as to the route.

The two villages consist of about thirty double tents, and the inhabitants call themselves Chopunnish or Piercednose.** The chief drew a chart of the river, and explained that a greater chief than himself, who governed this village and was called Twisted-hair, was now fishing at the distance of half a day's ride down the river. His chart made the Kooskooskee fork a little below his camp; a second fork was below; still further on, a large branch flowed in on each side, below which the river passed the mountains. Here was a great fall of water, near which lived white people, from whom were procured the white beads and brass ornaments worn by the women.

A chief of another band made a visit this morning, and smoked with Captain Clark. The hunters returned

---

* "I am very sick today and puke, which relieves me," Clark G. 121.
** Nez Perces Indians of the French, the leading tribe of the Shahaptian family of modern classification and nomenclature...
Latest returns of Shahaptian Indians are as follows:
1. Chopunnish, 1,515, on Nez Perces Reservation, Idaho.
2. Klikitat, perhaps half of 330 Indians on Yakama Reservation, Washington.
3. Paloos, census uncertain, on Yakama Reservation.
4. Tenaino, 69, Warm Springs Reservation, Oregon.
5. Tyigh, 430, with the Tenainos.
6. Umatilla, 179, on Umatilla Reservation, Oregon.
7. Walla-walla, 405, on Walla-walla Reservation, Oregon.

with-out having been able to kill anything. Captain Clark purchased as much dried salmon, roots, and berries as he could, with the articles he chanced to have in his pockets; and having sent them by one of the men and a hired Indian back to Captain Lewis, he went on toward the camp of Twisted hair. It was four o'clock before he set out, and the night soon came on; but having met an Indian coming from the river, they engaged him, by a present of a neck-cloth, to guide them to Twisted -hair's camp. For twelve miles they proceeded through the plain before they reached the river-hills, which are very high and steep. The whole valley from these hills to the Rocky Mountains is a beautiful level country, with a rich soil covered with grass. There is, however, but little timber, and the ground is badly watered. The plain is so much lower than the surrounding hills, or so much sheltered by them, that the weather is quite warm, while the cold of the mountains is extreme. From the top of the river -hills they proceeded down for three miles till they reached the water-side [Kooskooskee river, at the mouth of Village creek from the east*], near midnight. Here they found a small camp of five squaws and three children, the chief himself being camped, with two others, on a small island in the river; the guide called to him, and he soon came over. Captain Clark gave him a medal, and they smoked together till one o'clock.

---

* Clark G. 133, Sept. 21st: " N 80° W. 12 miles thro an open leavel rich pine country to the top of the river hills, passed no water. S. 70°. W. 3 miles clown a steep hill to the [Kooskooskee] river at the mouth of a small [village, now – Flores or Jim Ford's] creek on which the Indian village is situated " the camp of the Twisted hare," sic, Clark G 121. This creek is nameless in Clark G, and hence no name appears in Biddle; it is called Village creek in another codex.

We could not set out till eleven o'clock because, boing obliged in the evening to loosen our horses to enable them to find subsistence, it is always difficult to collect them in the morning. At that hour we continued along the ridge on which we had slept, and at one and a half miles reached a large creek running to our left just above its junction with one of its branches. We proceeded down the low grounds of this creek, which are level, wide, and heavily timbered; but turned to the right at the distance of two and a half miles, and began to pass the broken and hilly country; the thick timber had fallen in so many places that we could scarcely make our way. After going five miles, we passed the creek on which Captain Clark had camped during the night of the 19th, and continued five miles farther over the same kind of road, till we came to the forks of a large creek. We crossed the northern branch of this stream, and proceeded down it on the west side for a mile. Here we found a small plain, where there was tolerable grass for the horses, and therefore remained during the night, having made fifteen miles, on a course S. 30° W.*

The arbor vitae [*Thuja occidentalis*] increases in size and quantity as we advance, some of the trees we passed today being capable of forming periogues at least 45 feet in length. We were so fortunate also as to kill a few pheasants and a prairie-wolf, which, with the remainder of the horse, sup-plied us with one meal, the last of our provisions, our food for the morrow being wholly dependent on the chance of our guns.

---

* *Sic.* but read S. 80° W – See Clark's course of September 19th. The expedition is on his trail.

Sunday, September 22d. – Captain Clark passed over to the island with Twisted-hair, who seemed to be cheerful and sincere in his conduct. The river at this place is about one hundred and sixty yards wide, but interrupted by shoals; the low grounds on its borders are narrow. The hunters brought in three deer; after which Captain Clark left his party, and, accompanied by Twisted-hair and his son, rode back to the village, where he arrived about sunset. They then walked up together to the second village, where we had just arrived.

We had intended to set out early; but one of the men having neglected to hobble his horse, he strayed away, and we were obliged to wait till nearly twelve o'clock. We then proceeded on a western course for two and a half miles, when we met the hunters sent by Captain Clark from the village seven and a half miles distance, with provisions. This supply was most seasonable, as we had tasted nothing since last night; and the fish, roots, and berries, in addition to a crow which we had killed on the route, completely satisfied our hunger. After this refreshment we proceeded with much better spirits, and at a few miles were overtaken by the two men who had been sent back after a horse on the 20th. They were perfectly exhausted with the fatigue of walking and the want of food; but, as we had two spare horses, they were mounted and brought onto the village.

They had set out about three o'clock in the afternoon of the 20th, with one horse between them; after crossing the mountain, they came to the place where we had eaten the horse. Here they camped, and having no food made a fire and roasted the head of the horse, which even our appetites had spared, and supped on the ears, skin, and lips of the animal. The next morning, 21st, they found the track of the horse; pursuing it, they recovered the saddle-bags, and at length, about eleven o'clock, the horse himself. Being now both mounted, they set out to return, and slept at a small stream; during the day they had nothing at all except two pheasants, which were so torn to pieces by the shot that the head and legs were the only parts fit for food. In this situation they found the next morning, 22d, that during the night their horses had run away or been stolen by the Indians. They searched for them until nine o'clock, when, seeing they could not recover them and fearful of starvation if they remained where they were, they set out on foot to join us, carrying the saddle-bags alternately. They walked as fast as they could during the day, till they reached us in a deplorable state of weakness and inanition. As we approached the village most of the women, though apprised of our being expected, fled with their children into the neighboring woods. The men, however, received us without any apprehension, and gave us a plentiful supply of provisions. The plains were now crowded with Indians, who came to see the persons of the whites, and the strange things they brought with them; but, as our guide was a perfect stranger to their language, we could converse by signs only. Our inquiries were chiefly directed to the situation of the country, the courses of the rivers, and the Indian villages, of all of which we received information from several of the Indians; and as their accounts varied but little from each other, we were induced to place confidence in them. Among others, Twisted-hair drew a chart of the riv-

IN THE HEART OF THE BITTER-ROOT MOUNTAINS:
The Story of "the Carlin Hunting Party"

er on a white elk-skin. According to this, the Kooskooskee forks [confluence of its north fork] a few miles from this place; two days toward the south is an-other and larger fork [confluence of Snake river], on which the Shoshone or Snake Indians fish; five days' journey farther is a large river from the northwest [*i.e.*, the Columbia itself], into which Clark's river empties; from the mouth of that river [*i.e.* confluence of the Snake with the Columbia] to the falls is five days' journey farther; on all the forks as well as on the main river great numbers of Indians reside, and at the falls are establishments of whites [not so then]. This was the story of Twisted-hair.

Monday, September 23d. – The chiefs and warriors were all assembled this morning, and we explained to them where we came from, the objects of our visiting them, and our pacific intentions toward all the Indians. This being conveyed by signs, might not have been perfectly comprehended, but appeared to give perfect satisfaction. We now gave a medal to two of the chiefs, a shirt in addition to the medal already received by Twisted-hair, and delivered a flag and handkerchief for the grand chief on his return. To these were added a knife, a handkerchief, and a small piece of tobacco for each chief. The inhabitants did not give us any provisions gratuitously. We therefore purchased a quantity of fish, berries [chiefly red haws], and roots; and in the afternoon went on to the second village. Twisted-hair introduced us into his own tent, which consisted, however, of nothing more than pine-bushes and bark, and gave us some dried salmon boiled. We continued our purchases, and obtained as much provisions as our horses could carry in their present weak condition as far as the river. The men exchanged a few old canisters for dressed elk-skins, of which they made shirts. Great crowds of the natives were around us all night, but we have not yet missed anything, except a knife and a few other articles stolen yesterday from a shot-pouch. At dark we had a hard wind from the southwest accompanied with rain which lasted – half an hour; but in the morning,

September 24th. The weather was fair. We sent back Colter in search of the horses lost in the mountains, and having collected the rest set out at ten o'clock along the same route already passed by Captain Clark toward the river. All around the village the women are busily employed in gathering and dressing the pasheco-root, of which large quantities are heaped in piles over the plain. We now felt severely the consequence of eating heartily after our late privations. Captain Lewis and two of the men were taken very ill last evening; today he could hardly sit on his horse, while others were obliged to be put on horseback, and some, from extreme weakness and pain, were forced to lie down alongside of the road for some time. At sunset we reached the island where the hunters had been left on the 22d. They had been unsuccessful, having killed only two deer since that time, and two of them were very sick. A little below this island is a larger one on which we camped,* and administered Rush's pills to the sick.

September 25th. – The weather was very hot and oppressive to the party, most of whom are now complaining of sickness. Our situation, indeed, rendered it necessary

---

* In the Kooskooskee River, a mile or so above Rockdam or Oro Fino creek.

IN THE HEART OF THE BITTER-ROOT MOUNTAINS:
The Story of "the Carlin Hunting Party"

to husband our remaining strength, and it was determined to proceed down the river in canoes. Captain Clark, therefore, set out with Twisted-hair and two young men in quest of timber for canoes. As he went down the river* he crossed at the distance of a mile a creek from the right, which, from the rock which obstructed its passage, he called Rockdam River. The hills along the river are high and steep; the low grounds are narrow, and navigation of the river is embarrassed by two rapids. At the distance of three miles farther, he reached two nearly equal forks**

---

* Now called Oro Fino, in Spanish. This is the creek on one of whose. upper reaches is Pierce City, county seat of Shoshone County, Idaho.

** Confluence of the north fork of the Kooskooskee or Clearwater with this river itself. Clark G. 134, starting from Village [Flores] creek: "West 3 miles down the river to the mouth of a large creek I call rock Dam on the right side, passing a bad road on a steep hill side and the place the Indian catch fish at 2 Islands. River. about 150 yds. wide and is the one we killed the 1st Coalt on N 70° W. 2 miles down the Kosskosske River to a rapid at a graveley Island Hills high & Steep Small bottoms covered with pine passed 2 rapids. S, 75° W. 3 miles to the forks of the river. the N. W. fork as large as the [other, I call it the] Chopunnish, River. Crossed to the South Side and formed a camp to build Canoes &c In a Smal Pine bottom opposit a riffle in the South fok &c." That was a wonderful inference the great geographer drew that here again was the same river on which the first colt was killed – considering that he never saw it from Colt-killed creek to Village creek, and meanwhile crossed mountain after mountain, with creeks running both to the right and to the left. The total distance, from mouth of Traveler's rest creek to the present camp by one codex is 190 miles, by another 184; the crow-flight distance is very much less, because the trail is so crooked, both in the vertical and horizontal planes. Having been neither frozen nor starved quite to death – having survived camass roots, tartar emetic, and Rush's pills. the explorers have reached navigable Columbian waters, by riding and – eating their horses. They

of the river, one of which flowed in from the north. Here he rested for an hour and cooked a few salmon, which one of the Indians caught with his gig. Here he was joined by two canoes of Indians from below; they were long, steady, and loaded with the furniture and provisions of two families. He now crossed the south fork [main stream of the Clearwater or Kooskooskee], and returned to camp on the south side, through a narrow pine-bottom the greater part of the way, in which was found much fine timber for canoes. One of the Indian boats, with two men, set out at the same time; and such was their dexterity in managing the pole that they reached camp within fifteen minutes after him, though they had to drag the canoe over three rapids. He found Captain Lewis and several of the men still very sick; and distributed, to such as were in need of it, salts and tartar emetic.*

September 26th.** – Having resolved to go down to

---

call this place Canoe Camp, because they build boats here. We have them once more between river banks; by the grace of God, good luck, and especially good steering, the expedition will shoot every rapid without drowning anybody, down the Kooskooskee, down the Snake, and down the Columbia, to the Pacific Ocean.

* "I administered Salts, Pils, Galip, [jalap], Tartar emitic &c. " Clark G. 127. What the "and so forth" was the codex does not say; yet we know that but one man died during the expedition.

** Gass, p. 143, gives an interesting natural-history note at this date; "There appears to be a kind of sheep in this country, besides the ibex or mountain sheep [*Ovis montana*], which have wool on. I saw some of the skins, which the natives had, with wool four inches long, and as fine white and soft as any I had ever seen." This, of course, is the Rocky Mountain goat [*Haplocerus montanus*]. Putting ourselves back to 1805, we cannot wonder at the confusion that arose between these two animals, neither of which had at that time been recognized by science. It was a sufficiently

IN THE HEART OF THE BITTER-ROOT MOUNTAINS:
The Story of "the Carlin Hunting Party"

some spot calculated for building canoes, we set out early this morning, proceeded five miles, and camped on low ground on the south, opposite the forks of the river. But so weak were the men that several were taken sick in coming down, the weather being oppressively hot. Two chiefs and their families followed us, and camped with a great number of horses near us; soon after our arrival we were joined by two Indians, who came down the north fork on a raft. We purchased some fresh salmon, and having distributed axes and portioned – off the labor of the party, we began

Friday, 27th. At an early hour, the preparations for making five canoes. But few of the men, however, were able to work, and of these several were soon taken ill, as the day proved very hot. The hunters returned without any game, and seriously indisposed, so that nearly the whole party was now ill. We procured some fresh salmon, and Colter, who now returned with one of the horses, brought half a deer, which was very nourishing to the invalids. Several Indians from a camp below us came up to see us.

September 28th. – The men continue ill, though some of those first attacked are recovering. Their general complaint is a heaviness at the stomach, and a lax which is rendered more painful by the heat of the weather and the diet of fish and roots to which they are confined, as no game is to be procured. A number of Indians collect about us in the course of the day, to gaze at the strange appearance of everything – belonging to us.

---

perplexing case goats with wool mistaken for sheep, and sheep without wool mistaken for ibexes.

September 29th. Tho morning was cool, the wind from the southwest; but in the afternoon the heat returned. The men continue ill; but all those who are able to work are occupied at the canoes. The spirits of the party were much recruited by three deer brought in by the hunters.

September 30th. – The sick began to recruit their strength, the morning being fair and pleasant. The Indians pass in great numbers up and down the river, and we observe large quantities of small ducks going – down this morning Tuesday, October 1st, 1805. The morning was cool, the wind easterly; but the latter part of the day was warm. We were visited by several Indians from the tribe below, and others from the main south fork. To two of the most distinguished men we made presents of a ring and brooch, and to each of five others a piece of ribbon, a little tobacco, and the fifth part of a neck-cloth. We now dried our clothes and other articles, and selected some articles, such as the Indians admire, in order to purchase some provisions, as we have nothing left except a little dried fish, which operates – as a complete purgative.

October 2d. The day was very warm. Two men were sent to the village with a quantity of these articles to purchase food. We are now reduced to roots, which produce violent pains in the stomach. Our work continued as usual, and many of the party are convalescent. The hunters returned in the afternoon with nothing but a small prairie wolf; so that our provisions being exhausted, we killed one of the – horses to eat and provide soup for the sick.

October 3d. The fine cool morning and easterly wind had an agreeable effect upon the party, most of whom are now able to work.* The Indians from below left us, and we were visited – by others from different quarters.

October 4th. Again we had a cool east wind from the mountains. The men were now much better, and Captain Lewis himself has so far recovered as to walk about a little. Three Indians arrived today from the great [Snake] river to the south. The two men also returned from the village with roots and fish; and as the flesh of the horse killed yesterday was exhausted, we were confined to that diet, although it was unwholesome as well as unpleasant. The afternoon was warm.

October 5th. – The wind easterly and the weather cool. The canoes being finished, it became necessary to dispose of our horses. They were therefore collected, to the number of thirty-eight, and being branded and marked were delivered to three Indians, the two brothers and son of a chief, who promised to accompany us down the river. To each of these men we gave a knife and some small articles, and they agreed to take good care of the horses till our return. The hunters with all their diligence are unable to kill anything, the hills being high and rugged, and the woods too dry to hunt deer, which is the only game in the country. We therefore continue to eat dried fish and roots, which are purchased from the squaws by

---

* "All the men are now able to work; but the greater number are-very weak. To save them from hard labor – , we have adopted the Indian method of burning out the canoes." Gass, p. 144. Both the captains had suffered severely, and scarcely a man escaped diarrhoea or dysentery. They had come from snowy mountains, gaunt as famished wolves, into a sultry valley, and suddenly changed their. fare from scant rations of horseflesh to a full diet of fish and roots Taken in sufficient quantity, camass is. both emetic and purgative to those who are not accustomed to eat it.

means of small presents, chiefly white beads, of which they are extravagantly fond. Some of these roots seem to possess very active properties; for after supping on them this evening, we were swelled to such a degree as to be scarcely able to breathe for several hours. Toward night we launched two canoes, which – proved to be very good.

October 6th. This morning is again cool and the wind easterly. The general course of the wind seems to resemble that which we observed on the east side of the mountain. While on the headwaters of the Missouri we had every morning a cool wind from the west. At this place a cool breeze springs up during the latter part of the night, or near daybreak, and continues till seven or eight o'clock, when it subsides, and the latter part of the day is warm. Captain Lewis is not so well as he was, and Captain Clark was also taken ill. We buried all our saddles in a cache near the river, about one-half mile below, and deposited at the same time a canister of powder and a bag of balls. The time which could be spared from our labors on the canoes was devoted to some astronomical observations.* The latitude of our camp, as deduced from the mean of two observations, is 46° 34' 56" 3'" north.

October 7th. – This morning all the canoes were put in the water and loaded, the oars fixed, and every preparation made for setting out.** But when we were all

---

*   Given in full, Clark G – .129 and 136; others G. 138, 139. The latitude deduced is very close one of the best determinations made
** Canoe Camp, at junction of the north fork with the main stream, whence the expedition starts to-day, is at the point where the Kooskooskee is conventionally divided into " Upper and Lower." The latter course is about 40 miles; first 17 m. a little N. of W., then 9 m. about S. W., then nearly due W. to Lewiston at the con-

ready, the two chiefs who had promised to accompany us were not to be found, and at the same time we missed a pipe tomahawk. We therefore proceeded without them.* Below the forks this river is called Kooskooskee; it is a clear, rapid stream, with a number of shoals and difficult places. For Some miles the hills are steep and the low grounds narrow; then succeeds an open country, with a few trees scattered along the river. At the distance of nine miles is a small creek** on the left. We passed in the course of the day ten rapids, in descending which one of the canoes struck a rock and sprung a leak; we however continued for nineteen miles and camped on the left side of the river, opposite the mouth of a small run. Here the canoe was unloaded and repaired, and two lead canisters of powder were deposited. Several camps of Indians were on the sides of the river, but we had little intercourse with any of them.

---

fluence of the Kooskooskee with the Snake. The principal tributary in this course is Colter's or Potlatch creek, from the north; there are five or six others. Besides various cobblestone bars and minor "riffles," as they are called by the rivermen, several rapids obstruct the navigation of the river, as the expedition learns to its cost. Some of these are noted by name, beyond.

* "The morning of the 7th was pleasant, and we put the last of our canoes into the water; loaded them, and found that they carried all our baggage with convenience. We had four large canoes and one small one, to look ahead. About 3 o'clock in the afternoon we began our voyage down the river and found the rapids in some places very dangerous. One of our canoes sprung a leak. We thererefore halted and mended her, after going 20 miles."

** In fact there are two creeks, from the south or left, falling in close together. The upper one of these is now called Big Canyon creek: the lower, Jack's creek. At tonight's camp, the "small run" from the north, is Bedrock creek. Among rapids passed today are: Steamboat riffle, 500 feet long: Saddle-bag rapid, 400 feet; Big Eddy, 400 feet; and Tenpowwee, 1,000 feet or more.

APPENDIX G.

[NOTE. LEWIS and Clark passed the winter of 1805-6 on the shore of the Pacific Ocean, and being desirous of reaching civilization before the succeeding winter they started out early in the spring .on the return trip, reaching the Clearwater country again in May They passed through this region over practically the same route on their return; but much new matter and information concerning the rigorous climate, etc., is contained in their narrative, which is again taken up at that point.] –

May 7th, 1806. From the plain we observed that the spurs of the Rocky Mountains are still perfectly covered with snow, which the Indians inform us is so deep that we shall not be able to pass before the next full moon – that is, the 1st of June, though others place the time for crossing it at a still greater distance. To us, who are desirous of reaching the plains of the Missouri if for no other reason, for the purpose of enjoying a good meal – this intelligence was by no means welcome, and gave no relish to the remainder of the horse killed at Colter's Creek, which formed our supper, as part of which had already been our dinner.

June 8th – One of the Indians informed us that we could not pass the mountain before the next full moon, or about the 1st of July, because, if we attempted it before that time, the horses would be forced to travel without food three days on the top of the mountains. This intelligence was disagreeable, for it excited a doubt as to the most proper time for crossing the mountains; but having no time to lose, we are determined to risk the hazards, and start as soon as the Indians generally consider it practic-able, which is about the middle of this month.

June 16th. – We readily collected our horses, and having taken breakfast, proceeded at six o'clock up the [east-

IN THE HEART OF THE BITTER-ROOT MOUNTAINS:
The Story of "the Carlin Hunting Party"

erly branch of Collins] creek, through handsome meadows of fine grass, and a great abundance of quamash.

At the distance of two miles we crossed this creek, and ascended a ridge in a direction toward the northeast. Fallen timber still obstructed our way so much that it was eleven o'clock before we had made seven miles, to a small branch of Hungry Creek. In the hollows and on the north sides of the hills large quantities of snow still remain, in some places to the depth of two or three feet. Vegetation is proportionally retarded, the dog* tooth violet being just in bloom, and the honeysuckle, huckleberry, and a small species of white maple beginning to put forth their leaves. These appearances, in a part of the country comparatively low, are ill omens of the practicability of passing the mountains. But being determined to proceed, we halted* merely to take a hasty meal, while the horses were grazing, and then resumed our march. The route was through thick woods and over high hills, intersected by deep ravines and obstructed by fallen timber. We found much difficulty also in following the road, the greater part of it being covered with snow, which lies in great masses eight or ten feet deep, and would be impassable were it not so firm as to bear our horses. Early in the evening we reached Hungry Creek, at the place where Captain Clark had left a horse for us as we passed on Sept. 19th; and finding a small glade with some grass, though not enough for our horses, we thought it better to halt for the night,

---

* This nooning was at "a handsome little glade" on the "small branch" of Hungry creek, Lewis L. 44 – a statement which may help to identify the spot. This branch of. Hungry creek is named Fish creek on June 24th – see also June 18th The codex also. says that " this morning Windsor busted his rifle near the muzzle "

lest by going farther we should find nothing for the horses to eat. Hungry Creek is small at this place, but deep, and discharges a torrent of water, perfectly transparent and cold as ice. During the 15 miles of our route to-day, the principal timber was pitch-pine, white pine, larch, and fir. The long-leaved pine extends but a small distance on this side of Collins Creek, and the white cedar does not reach beyond the branch of Hungry Creek on which we dined. In the early part of the day we saw the columbine, the bluebell, and the yellow flowering-pea in bloom. There is also in these mountains a great quantity of angelica, stronger to the taste and more highly scented than that common in the United States. The smell is very pleasant, and the natives, after drying and cutting the plants into small pieces, wear them in strings around – their necks.

June 17th. We find lately that the air is pleasant in the course of the day; but notwithstanding the shortness of the night, it becomes very cold before morning. At an early hour we collected our horses and proceeded down the [Hungry] creek, which we crossed twice with much difficulty and danger, in consequence of its depth and rapidity. We avoided two other crossings of the same kind, by crossing over a steep and rocky hill. At the distance of seven miles the road begins the ascent to the main ridges which divide the waters of the Chopunnish and [main] Kooskooskee Rivers.* We followed it up a mountain for

---

* This is the first distinct statement in the text that the route is on a divide between the watershed northward of the north fork of the Kooskooskee and the main watershed southward. The outward route made it evident that they were on an extended divide, but what one the explorers could not.say, as they knew nothing of what was before them or on either hand.

IN THE HEART OF THE BITTER-ROOT MOUNTAINS:
The Story of "the Carlin Hunting Party"

about three miles, when we found ourselves enveloped in snow from twelve to fifteen feet in depth, even on the south side of the mountain, with the fullest exposure to the sun. Winter now presented itself in all its rigors; the air was keen and cold, no vestige of vegetation was to be seen, and our hands and feet benumbed.

We halted at the sight of this new difficulty. We already knew that to wait till the snows of the mountains had dissolved, so as to enable us to distinguish the road, would defeat our design of returning to the United States this season. We now found also that as the snow bore our horses very well, travelling was infinitely easier than it was last fall, when the rocks and fallen timber had so much obstructed our march. But it would require five days to reach the fish-weirs at the mouth of Colt [killed] Creek, even if we were able to follow the proper ridges of the mountains; and the danger of missing our direction is exceedingly great while every track is covered with snow. During these five days, too, we have no chance of finding either grass or underwood for our horses, the snow being so deep. To proceed, therefore, under such circumstances, would be to hazard our being bewildered in the mountains, and to insure the loss of our horses; even should we be so fortunate as to escape with our lives, we might be obliged to abandon all our papers and collections. It was therefore decided not to venture any further; to deposit here all the baggage and provisions for which we had no immediate use; and, reserving only subsistence for a few days, to return while our horses were yet strong to some spot where we might live by hunting, till a guide could be procured to conduct us across the mountains. Our baggage was placed

APPENDIX G.

on scaffolds and carefully covered, as were also the instruments and papers, which we thought it safer to leave than to risk over the roads and creeks by which we came.

Having completed this operation, we set out at one o'clock; and treading back our steps, reached Hungry Creek, which we ascended for two miles till, finding some scanty grass, we camped.* The rain fell during the greater

---

* Gass thus records this disheartening day, Tuesday, 17th: " We early continued our march; took down Hungry creek about six miles, and then took up a large mountain. When we got about half way up the mountain the ground was entirely covered with snow three feet deep; as we ascended it still became deeper, until we arrived at the top, where. it was twelve or fifteen feet deep; but it, in general, carried our horses Here there was not the appearance of a green shrub, or anything for our horses to subsist on; and we know it cannot be better-for four days' march, even could we find the road or course, which appears almost impossible, without a guide perfectly acquainted with the mountains. We therefore halted to determine what was best to be done, as it appeared not only imprudent but highly dangerous to proceed without a guide of any kind. After remaining about two hours we concluded it would be most advisable to go back to some place where there was food for our horses. We therefore hung up our loading on poles, tied to and extended between trees, covered it all safe with, deerskins and turned back melancholy and disappointed." There was perhaps no more critical day in the history of the expedition than this, and certainly none when the spirits of the party were at a lower ebb. The outlook was four or five days of ten to fifteen feet deep snow, no guide, no road, and no forage; it would have been madness to proceed; it was wisdom to retire from frowning "old Baldy."

Gass gives the mishaps of to-day tersely: "We started about eight o'clock and found the road very slippery and bad Two men went on ahead to the village to inquire for a guide., and two more remained to look for two horses that could not be found We proceeded on, with four men in front to cut some bushes out of the path; but did not go very far till one of the men cut himself very badly with a large knife; we had to halt and bind up his wound. We went again forward, and in crossing the creek

- 209 -

IN THE HEART OF THE BITTER-ROOT MOUNTAINS:
The Story of "the Carlin Hunting Party"

part of the evening, and as this was the first time that we have ever been compelled to make any retrograde movement, we feared that it might depress the spirits of the men; but though they were somewhat dejected at the circumstance, the obvious necessity precluded all repining.

During the night our horses straggled in search of food to a considerable distance among the thick timber on the hill-sides, nor could we collect them till nine o'clock the next morning.

June 18th. – Two of them were, however, still missing, and we therefore directed two of the party [Shields and Lepage] to remain and hunt for them. At the same time we dispatched Drewyer and Shannon to the Chopunnish [Indians], in the plains beyond the Kooskooskee, in order to hasten the arrival of those Indians who had promised to accompany us; or at any rate, to procure a guide to conduct us to Traveler's-rest [creek]. For this purpose they took a rifle, as a reward to any one who would engage to conduct us, with directions to increase the reward, if necessary, by an offer of two other guns, to be given immediately, and ten horses, at the falls of the Missouri.

We then resumed our route. In crossing Hungry Creek one of the horses fell and rolled over with the rider [Colter], who was driven for a considerable distance among the rocks; but he fortunately escaped without losing his gun or suffering any injury. Another of the men [Potts] was cut very badly, in a vein in the inner side of the leg, and we had great difficulty in stopping the blood.

---

the horse of one of our. men fell with him threw him off, hurt his leg and lost his blanket".

About one o'clock we halted for dinner at the glade, on a branch [Fish Creek] of Hungry Creek, where we had dined on the 16th inst. Observing much track of deer, we left two men [R. and J. Fields] at this place to hunt, and then proceeded to Collins Creek, where we camped 12 in a pleasant situation, at the upper end of the meadows, two miles above our camp of the 15th inst. The hunters were immediately sent out, but they returned without having killed anything, though they saw some few tracks of deer, very great appearance of bear, and what is of more importance, a number of what they thought were salmon-trout in the creek. We therefore hoped by means of these fish and other game to subsist at this place without returning to Quamash flats, which we are unwilling to do, since there is in these meadows [where we are now] great abundance of good food for our horses.

June 20th. – Determined as we now are to reach the United States, if possible, this winter, it would be destructive to wait till the snows have melted from the road. The snows have formed a hard, coarse bed without crust, on which the horses walk safely without slipping; the chief difficulty, therefore, is to find the road. In this we may be assisted by the circumstance that, though generally ten feet in depth, the snow has been thrown off by the thick and spreading branches of the trees, and from around the trunk; while the warmth of the trunk itself, acquired by the reflection of the sun, or communicated by natural heat of the earth, which is never frozen under these masses, has dissolved the snow so much that immediately at the roots its depth is not more than one or two feet. We therefore hope that the marks of the baggage rubbing against the trees may be still perceived; and we have decided, in case the guide cannot be procured, that one of us will take three or four of our most expert woodsmen, several of our best horses, and an ample supply of provisions, go on two days' journey in advance, and endeavor to trace the route by the marks of the Indian baggage on the trees, which we would then mark more distinctly with a tomahawk. When they should have reached two days' journey beyond Hungry Creek, two of the men were to be sent back to apprise the rest of their success, and if necessary to cause them to delay there; lest, by advancing too soon, they should be forced to halt where no food could be obtained for the horses.

June 24th. – Set out on a second attempt to cross the mountains. On reaching Collins Creek, we found only one of our men [Frazier], who informed us that a short time before he arrived there yesterday, the two Indians, tired of waiting, had set out, and the other four of our men [Gass, Wiser, and R. and J. Fields] had accompanied them as they were directed. After halting, we went on to Fish Creek, the branch of Hungry Creek, where we had slept on the 19th inst. Here we overtook two [Gass and Wiser] of the party who had gone on with the Indians, and had been fortunate enough to persuade them to wait for us. During their stay at Collins Creek, they [R. and J. Fields] had killed only a single deer, and of this they had been very liberal to the Indians, whom they were prevailing upon to remain; so that they were without provisions, and two [R. and J. Fields] of them had set out for another branch of Hungry Creek, where we shall meet them tomorrow.

In the evening the Indians, in order, as they said, to bring fair weather for our journey, set fire to the woods. As these consisted chiefly of tall fir- trees, with very numerous dried branches, the blaze was almost instantaneous; and as the flame mounted to the tops of the highest trees, it resembled – a splendid display of fireworks.

June 25th. One of our guides complained of being sick a symptom by no means pleasant, for sickness is generally with an Indian the pretext for abandoning an enterprise which he dislikes. He promised, however, to overtake us; we therefore left him with his two companions, and set out at an early hour. At eleven o'clock we halted for dinner at the [another*] branch of Hungry Creek, where we found our two men [R. and J. Fields], who had killed nothing. Here, too, we were joined rather unexpectedly by our guides, who now appeared disposed to be faithful to their engagements. The Indian was indeed really sick, and having no other covering than a pair of moccasins and an elk-skin dressed without the hair, we supplied him with a buffalo-robe. In the evening we arrived at Hungry Creek,

---

* This branch. appears to be nameless, and remains to be identified. Here Lewis L 58 has: "At this place I met with a plant the root of which the Shoshones eat. it is a small knob root, a good deel in flavor and consistency like the Jerusalem artichoke [*Helianthus tuberosus.*] it has two small oval smooth leaves placed opposite on either side of the peduncle just above the root, the scape is only about four inches long: is round and smooth, the roots of this plant formed one of those collections. of roots which Drewyer took from the Shoshones last summer," *i.e.*, August 22d.

and halted for the night about a mile and a half – below our camp of the 16th inst.

June 26th. Having collected our horses and taken breakfast, we set out at six o'clock; and pursuing our former route [of June 17th], at length began to ascend for the second time,* the ridge of mountains. Near the snowy region we killed two of the small black pheasant [*Dendragapus franklini*] and one of the speckled pheasant [the same species]. These birds generally inhabit the higher parts of the mountains, where they feed on the leaves of pines and firs; both of them seem solitary and silent birds, for we have never heard either of them make a noise in any situation, and the Indians inform us that they do not drum or produce a whirring sound with their wings [as do the ruffed grouse of the genus Bonasa]. On reaching the top of the mountain [N. E. of Hungry Creek, Lewis L. 59], we found our deposit [made June 17th] untouched. The snow in the neighborhood had melted nearly 4 feet since the 17th inst. By measuring it accurately and comparing it by a mark which we then made, the general depth we discover to have been 10 feet 10 inches, though in some places still greater; but at this time it is about 7 feet.

It required two hours to arrange our baggage and prepare a hasty meal, after which the guides urged us to set off, as we had a long ride to make before reaching a spot where there was grass for our horses. We mounted,

---

* The expedition has now been twelve days (since June 14th) back and — forth between Quamash flats and the mountains. They have meanwhile traversed the route three times east, west, and east again and now for the second time run up against the snowy barrier.

and, following their steps, sometimes crossed abruptly steep hills, then wound along their sides near tremendous precipices, where, had our horses slipped, we should have been lost irrecoverably. Our route lay on the ridgy mountains which separate the waters of the Kooskooskee and Chopunnish, above the heads of all the streams, so that we met no running water. The whole country was completely covered with snow, except that occasionally we saw a few square feet of earth at the roots of some trees around which the snow had dissolved. We passed our camp of September 18th [1805]; late in the evening reached the deserted [desired] spot, and camped near a good spring of water.* It was on the steep side of a mountain, with no wood and a fair southern aspect, from which the snow seems to have melted for about ten days, and given place to an abundant growth of young grass, resembling greensward. There is also another species of grass, not unlike a flag, with a broad succulent leaf, which is confined to the upper part of the highest mountains. It is a favorite food of the horses, but at present is either covered with snow or just making its appearance. There is a third plant peculiar to the same regions, a species of whortleberry. There are also large quantities of a species

---

* Gass notes Thursday 26th: "We had a foggy morning; proceeded on early, and found the banks of snow much decreased; at noon we arrived at the place where we had left our baggage and stores. The snow here had sunk twenty inches. We took some dinner, but there was nothing for our horses to eat. We. measured the depth of snow here, and found it ten feet ten inches We proceeded over some very steep tops of the mountains and deep snow: but the snow was not sc deep in the drafts between them; fortunately we got in the evening to the side of a hill where. the snow was gone, and there was very good grass for our horses".

IN THE HEART OF THE BITTER-ROOT MOUNTAINS:
The Story of "the Carlin Hunting Party"

of bear-grass, which, though it grows luxuriantly over all these mountains and preserves its verdure during – the whole winter, is never eaten by horses.

June 27th. Early the next morning we resumed our route over the heights and steep hills of the same great ridge. At eight miles' distance we reached an eminence where the Indians have raised a conic mound of stone, six or eight feet high, on which is fixed a pole made of pine, about fifteen feet long. Here we halted and smoked for some time at the request of the Indians, who told us that, in passing the mountains with their families, some men are usually sent on foot from this place to fish at the entrance of Colt [killed*] Creek, whence they rejoin the main party at the Quamash glade on the head of the Kooskooskee. From this elevated spot we have a commanding view of the surrounding mountains, which so completely enclose us, that, though we have once [in September, 1805] passed them, we almost despair of ever escaping from them without the assistance of the Indians. The marks on the trees, which had been our chief dependence, are much fewer and more difficult to be distinguished than we had supposed. But our guides traverse this trackless region with a kind of instinctive sagacity; they never hesitate, they are never embarrassed; and so undeviating is their step, that wherever the snow has disappeared, for even a hundred paces, we find the summer road. With their aid the snow is scarcely a disadvantage; for though we are

---

* Observe that the " Quamash glade" here in mention – one of the several similar spots of the same name – is the Summit Prairie of note 24. Lewis L. 61, says that the stone mound above mentioned was one mile short of their camp of September 17th – a good point made for the identification of the latter.

APPENDIX G.

often obliged to slip down, yet the fallen timber and the rocks, which are now covered, were much more troublesome when we passed in the autumn. Travelling is indeed comparatively pleasant, as well as more rapid, the snow being hard and coarse, without a crust, and perfectly hard enough to prevent the horses sinking more than two or three inches. After the sun has been on it for some hours it becomes softer than it is early in the morning; yet they are almost always able to get a sure foothold.

After some time we resumed our route, and at the distance of three miles descended a steep mountain; then crossing two branches of the Chopunnish river, just above their forks, we began to mount a second ridge. Along this we proceeded for some time, and then, at the distance of seven miles, reached our camp of the 16th of September [1805*]. Near this place we crossed three small branches of the Chopunnish, and then ascended a second dividing ridge, along which we continued for nine miles, when the ridge became somewhat lower, and we halted for the night in a position similar to that of our camp last evening.

We had now travelled twenty-eight miles without taking the loads from our horses or giving them anything to eat, and as the snow where we halted had not much

---

* Streams previously noted as passing to the explorer's then right hand, *i.e.,* northward, are here again in mention, and now regarded, no-doubt correctly., as affluents of the Chopunnish or north fork of the Kooskooskee Yet on no contemporaneous- map I have seen does a single such tributary touch the Lo Lo trail. It is true that the Stevens No. 3, which dots in the 1864 Mullan trail, lays down several such northward-streams, but these are. only charted at their heads, without any connections lower down Lewis and Clark's trail in these mountains should be carefully studied in the making of the future correct map of Idaho.

dissolved there was still but little grass. Among the vegetation we observed great quantities of the white lily* with reflected petals, which is now in bloom, and in the same forwardness as it was in the plains on the 10th of May. As for ourselves, the whole stock of meat being gone, we distributed to each mess a pint of bear's oil, which, with boiled roots, made an agreeable dish. We saw several black-tailed or mule-deer [*Cariacus macrotis*], but could not get a shot at them, and were informed that there is an abundance of elk in the valley near the fishery on the Kooskooskee. The Indians also assert that on the mountains to our right are large numbers of what they call white buffalo or mountain sheep [*Haplocerus montanus*].

June 28th. Our horses strayed to some distance to look for food, and in the morning, when they were brought up, exhibited rather a gaunt appearance. The Indians, howeverer, promised that we should reach some good grass at noon, and we therefore set out after an early breakfast. Our route lay along the dividing ridge and across a very deep hollow, till at the distance of six miles we passed our camp of the 15th of September [1805]. A mile and a half farther we passed the road from the right, immediately on the dividing ridge, leading by the fishery. We went on, as we had done during the former part of the route, over deep snows; when, having made thirteen miles, we reached the side of a mountain just above the fishery;

---

* "Yellow lilly," Lewis L. 62. Codex also notes: "Potts'legg, which has been much swollen and inflamed for several days, is much better this evening and gives him but little pain. We applied the pounded roots and leaves of the wild ginger, from which he found great relief."

from which, having no timber, and a southern exposure, the snow had disappeared, leaving an abundance of fine grass. Our horses were very hungry as well as fatigued, and as there was no other spot within reach this evening where we could find any food for them, we determined to camp, though it was not yet midday. But as there was no water in the neighborhood, we melted snow for cooking.

Sunday, June 29th.* We continued along the ridge which we had been following for several days, till at the end of five miles it terminated; and bidding adieu to the snows in which we had been imprisoned, we descended to the main branch of the Kooskooskee. On reaching the water-side, we found a deer which had been left for us by two hunters who had been dispatched at an ea hour to the warm springs, and which proved a very seasonable addition to our food; for having neither meat nor oil, we were reduced to a diet of roots, without salt or any other addition. At this place, about a mile and a half from the spot where Quamash** Creek falls in from the northeast, the Kooskooskee is about thirty yards wide, and runs with great velocity over a bed which, like those of all the mountain streams, is composed of pebbles. We forded the

---

* Clark Q. 165. This date describes the "lady-slipper or mockerson flower.it is in shape and appearance much like ours [*i.e.,* a common orchid of the genus *Cyprepedium*], only that the corrolla is white. marked with small reins of a pale red longitudinally.on the inner side " This species is *Cypripedium montanum.*

** Here a new name for the Glade creek of notes 24 and 23 – see there. The Quamash flats about to be mentioned in this paragraph are the same as the Quamash glade of June 27th, but of course. not .the flats named-Quamash which were finally left on June 24th Lewis L 35 notes that to day's nooning was two miles past the camp of September 18th.

river and ascended for two miles the steep acclivities of a mountain, on the summit of which we found coming in from the right the old road which we had passed on our route last autumn. It was now much plainer and more beaten, which the Indians told us was owing to the frequent visits of the Ootlahshoots from the valley of Clark's River to the fishery, though there was no appearance of their having been here this spring.

www.ingramcontent.com/pod-product-compliance
Lightning Source LLC
LaVergne TN
LVHW051551070426
835507LV00021B/2521